PRIVACY AND IDENTITY PROTECTION

FEDERAL CYBERSECURITY

IDENTIFICATION AND MITIGATION EFFORTS OF SECTOR-SPECIFIC AGENCIES

PRIVACY AND IDENTITY PROTECTION

Additional books in this series can be found on Nova's website under the Series tab.

Additional e-books in this series can be found on Nova's website under the eBooks tab.

PRIVACY AND IDENTITY PROTECTION

FEDERAL CYBERSECURITY

IDENTIFICATION AND MITIGATION EFFORTS OF SECTOR-SPECIFIC AGENCIES

JEFFERY H. MATTHEWS
EDITOR

NOVINKA
New York

Library of Congress Cataloging-in-Publication Data

ISBN: 978-1-63485-310-1

Published by Nova Science Publishers, Inc. † New York

CONTENTS

PREFACE

U. S. critical infrastructures, such as financial institutions, commercial buildings, and energy production and transmission facilities, are systems and assets, whether physical or virtual, vital to the nation's security, economy, and public health and safety. To secure these systems and assets, federal policy and the National Infrastructure Protection Plan (NIPP) establish responsibilities for federal agencies designated as Sector-specific agencies (SSAs), including leading, facilitating, or supporting the security and resilience programs and associated activities of their designated critical infrastructure sectors. The objectives of this book are to determine the extent to which SSAs have identified the significance of cyber risks to their respective sectors' networks and industrial control systems; taken actions to mitigate cyber risks within their respective sectors; collaborated across sectors to improve cybersecurity; and established performance metrics to monitor improvements in their respective sectors.

In: Federal Cybersecurity
Editor: Jeffery H. Matthews
ISBN: 978-1-63485-310-1

Chapter 1

CRITICAL INFRASTRUCTURE PROTECTION: SECTOR-SPECIFIC AGENCIES NEED TO BETTER MEASURE CYBERSECURITY PROGRESS*

United States Government Accountability Office

WHY GAO DID THIS STUDY

U. S. critical infrastructures, such as financial institutions, commercial buildings, and energy production and transmission facilities, are systems and assets, whether physical or virtual, vital to the nation's security, economy, and public health and safety. To secure these systems and assets, federal policy and the National Infrastructure Protection Plan (NIPP) establish responsibilities for federal agencies designated as Sector-specific agencies (SSAs), including leading, facilitating, or supporting the security and resilience programs and associated activities of their designated critical infrastructure sectors.

GAO's objectives were to determine the extent to which SSAs have (1) identified the significance of cyber risks to their respective sectors' networks and industrial control systems, (2) taken actions to mitigate cyber risks within their respective sectors, (3) collaborated across sectors to improve cybersecurity, and (4) established performance metrics to monitor

* This is an edited, reformatted and augmented version of the United States Government Accountability Office publication, GAO-16-79, dated November 2015.

improvements in their respective sectors. To conduct the review, GAO analyzed policy, plans, and other documentation and interviewed public and private sector officials for 8 of 9 SSAs with responsibility for 15 of 16 sectors.

What GAO Recommends

GAO recommends that certain SSAs collaborate with sector partners to develop performance metrics and determine how to overcome challenges to reporting the results of their cyber risk mitigation activities. Four of these agencies concurred with GAO's recommendation, while two agencies did not comment on the recommendations.

What GAO Found

Sector-specific agencies (SSA) determined the significance of cyber risk to networks and industrial control systems for all 15 of the sectors in the scope of GAO's review. Specifically, they determined that cyber risk was significant for 11 of 15 sectors. Although the SSAs for the remaining four sectors had not determined cyber risks to be significant during their 2010 sector-specific planning process, they subsequently reconsidered the significance of cyber risks to the sector. For example, commercial facilities sector–specific agency officials stated that they recognized cyber risk as a high-priority concern for the sector as part of the updated sector planning process. SSAs and their sector partners are to include an overview of current and emerging cyber risks in their updated sector- specific plans for 2015.

SSAs generally took actions to mitigate cyber risks and vulnerabilities for their respective sectors. SSAs developed, implemented, or supported efforts to enhance cybersecurity and mitigate cyber risk with activities that aligned with a majority of actions called for by the National Infrastructure Protection Plan (NIPP). SSAs for 12 of the 15 sectors had not identified incentives to promote cybersecurity in their sectors as proposed in the NIPP; however, the SSAs are participating in a working group to identify appropriate incentives. In addition, SSAs for 3 of 15 sectors had not yet made significant progress in advancing cyber-based research and development within their sectors because it had not been an area of focus for their sector. Department of Homeland Security guidance for updating the sector-specific plans directs the SSAs to incorporate the NIPP's actions to guide their cyber risk mitigation activities, including cybersecurity-related actions to identify incentives and promote research and development.

All SSAs that GAO reviewed used multiple public-private and cross-sector collaboration mechanisms to facilitate the sharing of cybersecurity-related information. For example, the SSAs used councils of federal and nonfederal stakeholders, including coordinating councils and cybersecurity and industrial control system working groups, to coordinate with each other. In addition, SSAs participated in the National Cybersecurity and Communications Integration Center, a national center at the Department of Homeland Security, to receive and disseminate cyber-related information for public and private sector partners.

The Departments of Defense, Energy, and Health and Human Services established performance metrics for their three sectors. However, the SSAs for the other 12 sectors had not developed metrics to measure and report on the effectiveness of all of their cyber risk mitigation activities or their sectors' cybersecurity posture. This was because, among other reasons, the SSAs rely on their private sector partners to voluntarily share information needed to measure efforts. The NIPP directs SSAs and their sector partners to identify high-level outcomes to facilitate progress towards national goals and priorities. Until SSAs develop performance metrics and collect data to report on the progress of their efforts to enhance the sectors' cybersecurity posture, they may be unable to adequately monitor the effectiveness of their cyber risk mitigation activities and document the resulting sector-wide cybersecurity progress.

ABBREVIATIONS

CIPAC	Critical Infrastructure Partnership Advisory Council
CSCSWG	Cross-Sector Cybersecurity Working Group
DHS	Department of Homeland Security
DOD	Department of Defense
DOE	Department of Energy
DOT	Department of Transportation
EPA	Environmental Protection Agency
FBIIC	Financial and Banking Information Infrastructure Committee
FDA	Food and Drug Administration

FSLC	Federal Senior Leadership Council
GCC	government coordinating council
HHS	Department of Health and Human Services
ICS-CERT	Industrial Control Systems Cyber Emergency Response Team
ICSJWG	Industrial Control Systems Joint Working Group
NCCIC	National Cybersecurity and Communications Integration Center
NICC	National Infrastructure Coordinating Center
NIPP	National Infrastructure Protection Plan
NIST	National Institute of Standards and Technology
OCIA	Office of Cyber and Infrastructure Analysis
PPD	presidential policy directive
SSA	sector-specific agency
TSA	Transportation Security Administration
US-CERT	U.S. Computer Emergency Readiness Team
USDA	U.S. Department of Agriculture

***

November 19, 2015

The Honorable Michael McCaul
Chairman
The Honorable Bennie G. Thompson
Ranking Member
Committee on Homeland Security
House of Representatives

The nation's critical infrastructure provides the essential services–such as banking, water, and electricity–that underpin American society, and it relies extensively on computerized systems and electronic data to carry out its missions.[1] The cyber threat to critical infrastructure continues to grow and represents a serious national security challenge. Foreign malicious actors have directly attacked and extracted highly sensitive materials from the networks of government agencies and major critical infrastructure companies. To address the threat, a proactive and coordinated effort is necessary to strengthen and maintain secure, functioning, and resilient critical infrastructure–including privately owned or operated assets, networks, and systems–that are vital to public confidence and the nation's security, economy, health, and safety.

Due to the cyber-based threats to federal systems and critical infrastructure, the persistent nature of information security vulnerabilities, and the associated risks, we continue to designate information security as a government-wide high-risk area in our most recent biennial report to Congress, a designation we have made in each report since 1997.[2] In 2003, we expanded this high-risk area to include the protection of critical cyber infrastructure and we continued to do so in the most recent update to our high-risk list.

Federal policy and public-private plans establish various mechanisms for the development of public-private partnerships to help secure critical infrastructure. For example, the National Infrastructure Protection Plan (NIPP)[3] calls for efforts to be carried out through the joint efforts of multiple components of a partnership model, including federal agencies, referred to as "sector-specific agencies" (SSA), that are to serve as a federal interface for the prioritization and coordination of security and resilience efforts and to carry out incident management responsibilities for their assigned critical infrastructure sectors. Presidential Policy Directive 21 (PDD-21), among other things, identified 16 critical infrastructure sectors and designated associated federal SSAs.[4]

At your request, we reviewed the cybersecurity efforts of SSAs within their sectors and across sectors. Our objectives were to determine the extent to which SSAs have (1) identified the significance of cyber risks to their respective sectors' networks and industrial control systems, (2) taken actions to mitigate cyber risks within their respective sectors, (3) collaborated across sectors to improve cybersecurity, and (4) established performance metrics to monitor improvements in their respective sectors.

To conduct our evaluation, we analyzed relevant critical infrastructure protection policies and guidance for improving the cybersecurity posture of the nation's critical infrastructure. Based on these analyses, we identified nine federal departments and agencies designated as the SSA for a critical infrastructure sector. For this review, we focused on eight of the nine SSAs responsible for 15 of the 16 critical infrastructure sectors. We included the 15 sectors that involve private sector stakeholders in the SSAs' efforts to implement activities to address sector security and resiliency goals.[5]

To determine the extent to which SSAs identified the significance of cyber risks to their respective sectors, we reviewed the risk assessment methodologies employed by each SSA, as documented in the 2010 sector-specific plans, and other supplementary documentation such as formal risk assessment documents. To determine the extent of SSAs' activities to mitigate cyber risks, we compared sector-specific planning documents and actions against 10 of 12 efforts called for in the 2013 NIPP that we determined to have a cybersecurity nexus. To determine the extent of the sector-specific agencies' collaborative efforts to enhance their sectors' cybersecurity environment, we identified the collaborative councils and working groups that SSAs used to share cybersecurity- related information within and across the sectors. To identify performance measures implemented for sector-specific agencies to monitor cybersecurity in their respective sectors, we analyzed annual reports and other performance reporting documents. Additionally, we reviewed past sector annual reports, which tracked actions of the sector against goals established in the 2010 sector-specific plans.

For the four objectives, we also interviewed federal officials from the eight SSAs regarding activities such as their efforts to identify cybersecurity risks to their respective critical infrastructure sectors, mitigate such risk, collaborate across sectors on cybersecurity-related issues, and measure the progress of sectors and the effectiveness of their effort. In addition, to confirm federal efforts and better understand the roles and responsibilities of the SSAs, we collected and analyzed relevant documents and interviewed private sector stakeholders from the 15 identified critical infrastructure sectors.

We conducted this performance audit from June 2014 to November 2015 in accordance with generally accepted government auditing standards. Those standards require that we plan and perform the audit to obtain sufficient, appropriate evidence to provide a reasonable basis for our findings and conclusions based on our audit objectives. We believe that the evidence obtained provides a reasonable basis for our findings and conclusions based on our audit objectives. Appendix I discusses our objectives, scope, and methodology in greater detail.

BACKGROUND

U. S. critical infrastructure is made of systems and assets, whether physical or virtual, so vital to the United States that the incapacity or destruction of such systems and assets would have a debilitating impact on the nation's security, national economic security, national public health or safety, or any combination of these matters. Critical infrastructure includes, among other things, banking and financing institutions, telecommunications networks, and energy production and transmission facilities, most of which are owned and operated by the private sector. Sector-specific agencies (SSA) are federal departments or agencies with responsibility for providing institutional knowledge and specialized expertise as well as leading, facilitating, or supporting the security and resilience programs and associated activities of its designated critical infrastructure sector in the all-hazards[6] environment.

The Nation Faces an Evolving Array of Cyber-Based Threats

Threats to systems supporting critical infrastructure are evolving and growing. Cyber threats can be unintentional or intentional. Unintentional or non-adversarial threats include equipment failures, software coding errors, and the actions of poorly trained employees. They also include natural disasters and failures of critical infrastructure on which the organization depends but are outside of its control. Intentional threats include both targeted and untargeted attacks from a variety of sources, including criminal groups, hackers, disgruntled employees, foreign nations engaged in espionage and information warfare, and terrorists. These threat adversaries vary in terms of the capabilities of the actors, their willingness to act, and their motives, which can include seeking monetary gain or seeking an economic, political, or military advantage. Table 1 describes the sources of cyber-based threats in more detail.

Cyber threat adversaries make use of various techniques, tactics, and practices, or exploits, to adversely affect an organization's computers, software, or networks, or to intercept or steal valuable or sensitive information. These exploits are carried out through various conduits, including websites, e-mail, wireless and cellular communications, Internet protocols, portable media, and social media. Further, adversaries can leverage common computer software programs, such as Adobe Acrobat and Microsoft Office, to deliver a threat by embedding exploits within software files that can be activated when a user opens a file within its corresponding program. Table 2 provides descriptions of common exploits or techniques, tactics, and practices used by cyber adversaries.

Reports of cyber exploits illustrate the debilitating effects such attacks can have on the nation's security, economy, and on public health and safety.

- In May 2015, media sources reported that data belonging to 1.1 million health insurance customers in the Washington, D.C., area were stolen in a cyber attack on a private insurance company.

Attackers accessed a database containing names, birth dates, e-mail addresses, and subscriber ID numbers of customers.

Table 1. Common Cyber Threat Sources

Source	Description
Non-adversarial/non-malicious	
Failure in information technology equipment	Failures in displays, sensors, controllers, and information technology hardware responsible for data storage, processing, and communications
Failure in environmental controls	Failures in temperature/humidity controllers or power supplies
Software coding errors	Failures in operating systems, networking, and general-purpose and mission-specific applications
Natural or man-made disaster	Events beyond an entity's control such as fires, floods/tsunamis, tornadoes, hurricanes, and earthquakes
Unusual or natural event	Natural events beyond the entity's control that are not considered to be disasters (e.g., sunspots)
Infrastructure failure or outage	Failure or outage of telecommunications or electrical power
Unintentional user errors	Failures resulting from erroneous, accidental actions taken by individuals (both system users and administrators) in the course of executing their everyday responsibilities
Adversarial	
Hackers or hacktivists	Hackers break networks for the challenge, revenge, stalking, or monetary gain, among other reasons. Hacktivists are ideologically motivated actors who use cyber exploits to further political goals.
Malicious insiders	Insiders (e.g., disgruntled organization employees, including contractors) may not need a great deal of knowledge about computer intrusions because their position within the organization often allows them to gain unrestricted access and cause damage to the targeted system or to steal system data. These individuals engage in purely malicious activities and should not be confused with non-malicious insider accidents.
Nations	Nations, including nation-state, state-sponsored, and state-sanctioned programs, use cyber tools as part of their information-gathering and espionage activities. In addition, several nations are aggressively working to develop information warfare doctrine, programs, and capabilities.
Criminal groups and organized crime	Criminal groups seek to attack systems for monetary gain. Specifically, organized criminal groups use cyber exploits to commit identity theft, online fraud, and computer extortion.
Terrorist	Terrorists seek to destroy, incapacitate, or exploit critical infrastructures in order to threaten national security, cause mass casualties, weaken the economy, and damage public morale and confidence.
Unknown malicious outsiders	Unknown malicious outsiders are threat sources or agents that, due to a lack of information, agencies are unable to classify as being one of the five types of threatsources or agents listed above.

Source: GAO analysis of unclassified government and nongovernment data. | GAO-16-79

Table 2. Common Methods of Cyber Exploits

Exploit	Description
Watering hole	A method by which threat actors exploit the vulnerabilities of carefully selected websites frequented by users of the targeted system. Malware is then injected to the targeted system via the compromised websites.
Phishing and spear phishing	A digital form of social engineering that uses authentic-looking e-mails, websites, or instant messages to get users to download malware, open malicious attachments, or open links that direct them to a website that requests information or executes malicious code.
Credentials based	An exploit that takes advantage of a system's insufficient user authentication and/or any elements of cyber-security supporting it, to include not limiting the number of failed login attempts, the use of hard-coded credentials, and the use of a broken or risky cryptographic algorithm.
Trusted third parties	An exploit that takes advantage of the security vulnerabilities of trusted third parties to gain access to an otherwise secure system.
Classic buffer overflow	An exploit that involves the intentional transmission of more data than a program's input buffer can hold, leading to the deletion of critical data and subsequent execution of malicious code.
Cryptographic weakness	An exploit that takes advantage of a network employing insufficient encryption when either storing or transmitting data, enabling adversaries to read and/or modify the data stream.
Structured Query Language (SQL) injection	An exploit that involves the alteration of a database search in a web-based application, which can be used to obtain unauthorized access to sensitive information in a database, resulting in data loss or corruption, denial of service, or complete host takeover.
Operating system command injection	An exploit that takes advantage of a system's inability to properly neutralize special elements used in operating system commands, allowing the adversaries to execute unexpected commands on the system by either modifying already evoked commands or evoking their own.
Cross-site scripting	An exploit that uses third-party web resources to run lines of programming code (referred to as scripts) within the victim's web browser or scriptable application. This occurs when a user, using a browser, visits a malicious website or clicks a malicious link. The most dangerous consequences can occur when this method is used to exploit additional vulnerabilities that may permit an adversary to steal cookies (data exchanged between a web server and a browser), log key strokes, capture screen shots, discover and collect network information, or remotely access and control the victim's machine.
Cross-site request forgery	An exploit that takes advantage of an application that cannot, or does not, sufficiently verify whether a well-formed, valid, consistent request was intentionally provided by the user who submitted the request, tricking the victim into executing a falsified request that results in the system or data being compromised.

Table 2. (Continued)

Exploit	Description
Path traversal	An exploit that seeks to gain access to files outside of a restricted directory by modifying the directory pathname in an application that does not properly neutralize special elements (e.g. '…', '/', '…/', etc.) within the pathname.
Integer overflow	An exploit where malicious code is inserted that leads to unexpected integer overflow, or wraparound, which can be used by adversaries to control looping or make security decisions in order to cause program crashes, memory corruption, or the execution of arbitrary code via buffer overflow.
Uncontrolled format string	Adversaries manipulate externally-controlled format strings in print-style functions to gain access to information and/or execute unauthorized code or commands.
Open redirect	An exploit where the victim is tricked into selecting a URL (website location) that has been modified to direct them to an external, malicious site which may contain malware that can compromises the victim's machine.
Heap-based buffer overflow	Similar to classic buffer overflow, but the buffer that is overwritten is allocated in the heap portion of memory, generally meaning that the buffer was allocated using a memory allocation routine, such as "malloc ()".
Unrestricted upload of files	An exploit that takes advantage of insufficient upload restrictions, enabling adversaries to upload malware (e.g., .php) in place of the intended file type (e.g., .jpg).
Inclusion of functionality from un-trusted sphere	An exploit that uses trusted, third-party executable functionality (e.g., web widget or library)as a means of executing malicious code in software whose protection mechanisms are unable to determine whether functionality is from a trusted source, modified in transit, or being spoofed.
Certificate and certificate authority compromise	Exploits facilitated via the issuance of fraudulent digital certificates (e.g., transport layer security and Secure Socket Layer). Adversaries use these certificates to establish secure connections with the target organization or individual by mimicking a trusted third party.
Hybrid of others	An exploit which combines elements of two or more of the aforementioned techniques.

Source: GAO analysis of unclassified government and nongovernment data. | GAO-16-79

- In December 2014, the Industrial Control Systems Cyber Emergency Response Team (ICS-CERT)[7] issued an updated alert on a sophisticated malware campaign compromising numerous industrial control system environments. Their analysis indicated that this campaign had been ongoing since at least 2011.

- In the January 2014 to April 2014 release of its Monitor Report, ICS-CERT reported that a public utility had been compromised when a sophisticated threat actor gained unauthorized access to its control system network through a vulnerable remote access capability configured on the system. The incident highlighted the need to evaluate security controls employed at the perimeter and ensure that potential intrusion vectors are configured with appropriate security controls, monitoring, and detection capabilities.

Federal Guidance Establishes Specific Roles and Responsibilities for Protecting the Nation's Critical Infrastructure

Federal policy and public-private plans establish roles and responsibilities for federal agencies working with the private sector and other entities to enhance the cyber and physical security of public and private critical infrastructures. These include PPD-21 and the NIPP.

PPD-21 shifted the nation's focus from protecting critical infrastructure against terrorism toward protecting and securing critical infrastructure and increasing its resilience against all hazards, including natural disasters, terrorism, and cyber incidents. The directive identified 16 critical infrastructure sectors and designated associated federal SSAs. Table 3 shows the 16 critical infrastructure sectors and the SSA for each sector.

PPD-21 identified SSA roles and responsibilities to include

- collaborating with critical infrastructure owners and operators; independent regulatory agencies, where appropriate; and with state, local, tribal, and territorial entities as appropriate;
- serving as a day-to-day federal interface for the prioritization and coordination of sector-specific activities;
- carrying out incident management responsibilities consistent with statutory authority and other appropriate policies, directives, or regulations; and
- providing, supporting, or facilitating technical assistance and consultations for their respective sector to identify vulnerabilities and help mitigate incidents, as appropriate.

Table 3. Critical Infrastructure Sectors and Related Sector-Specific Agency

Critical infrastructure sector	Description	Sector-specific agency
Chemical	Transforms natural raw materials into commonly used products benefiting society's health, safety, and productivity. The chemical sector produces products that are essential to automobiles, pharmaceuticals, food supply, electronics, water treatment, health, construction, and other necessities.	Department of Homeland Security (DHS)
Commercial facilities	Includes prominent commercial centers, office buildings, sports stadiums, theme parks, and other sites where large numbers of people congregate to pursue business activities, conduct personal commercial transactions, or enjoy recreational pastimes.	DHS
Communications	Provides wired, wireless, and satellite communications to meet the needs of businesses and governments.	DHS
Critical manufacturing	Transforms materials into finished goods. The sector includes the manufacture of primary metals, machinery, electrical equipment, appliances, and components, and transportation equipment.	DHS
Dams	Manages water retention structures, including levees, dams, navigation locks, canals (excluding channels), and similar structures, including larger and nationally symbolic dams that are major components of other critical infrastructures that provide electricity and water.	DHS
Defense industrial base	Supplies the military with the means to protect the nation by producing weapons, aircraft, and ships and providing essential services, including information technology and supply and maintenance.	Department of Defense
Emergency services	Saves lives and property from accidents and disaster. This sector includes fire, rescue, emergency medical services, and law enforcement organizations.	DHS
Energy	Provides the electric power used by all sectors and the refining, storage, and distribution of oil and gas. The sector is divided into electricity and oil and natural gas.	Department of Energy
Financial services	Provides the financial infrastructure of the nation. This sector consists of institutions like commercial banks, credit unions, insurance companies, mutual funds, government-sponsored enterprises, pension funds, and other financial institutions that carry out transactions.	Department of the Treasury

Critical infrastructure sector	Description	Sector-specific agency
Food and agriculture	Ensures the safety and security of food, animal feed, and food-producing animals; coordinates animal and plant disease and pest response; and provides nutritional assistance.	U.S. Department of Agriculture Department of Health and Human Services (Food and Drug Administration)
Government facilities	Ensures continuity of functions for facilities owned and leased by the government, including all federal, state, territorial, local, and tribal government facilities located in the United States and abroad.	DHS General Services Administration
Health care and public health	Protects the health of the population before, during, and after disasters and attacks. The sector consists of direct health care, health plans and payers, pharmaceuticals, laboratories, blood, medical materials, health information technology, mortuary care, and public health.	Department of Health and Human Services
Information technology	Produces information technology and includes hardware manufacturers, software developers, and service providers, as well as the Internet as a key resource.	DHS
Nuclear reactors, materials, and waste	Provides nuclear power. The sector includes commercial nuclear reactors and non-power nuclear reactors used for research, testing, and training; nuclear materials used in medical, industrial, and academic settings; nuclear fuel fabrication facilities; the decommissioning of reactors; and the transportation, storage, and disposal of nuclear materials and waste.	DHS
Transportation systems	Enables movement of people and assets that are vital to our economy, mobility, and security with the use of aviation, ships, rail, pipelines, highways, trucks, buses, and mass transit.	DHS (Transportation Security Administration and U.S. Coast Guard) Department of Transportation
Water and wastewater systems	Provides sources of safe drinking water from community water systems and properly treated wastewater from publicly owned treatment works.	Environmental Protection Agency

Source: GAO analysis of PPD 21. | GAO-16-79

The NIPP is to provide the overarching approach for integrating the nation's critical infrastructure protection and resilience activities into a single national effort. DHS developed the NIPP in collaboration with public and private sector owners and operators and federal and nonfederal government representatives, including sector-specific agencies, from the critical infrastructure community. It details DHS's roles and responsibilities in protecting the nation's critical infrastructures and how sector stakeholders should use risk management principles to prioritize protection activities within and across sectors. It emphasizes the importance of collaboration, partnering, and voluntary information sharing among DHS and industry owners and operators, and state, local, and tribal governments. The NIPP also stresses a partnership approach among the federal and state governments and industry stakeholders for developing, implementing, and maintaining a coordinated national effort to manage the risks to critical infrastructure and work toward enhancing physical and cyber resilience and security.

According to the NIPP, SSAs are to work with their private sector counterparts to understand cyber risk and develop sector-specific plans that address the security of the sector's cyber and other assets and functions. The SSAs and their private sector partners are to update their sector-specific plans based on DHS guidance to the sectors. The currently available sector-specific plans were released in 2010 to support the 2009 version of the NIPP.[8] In response to the most recent NIPP, released in December 2013, DHS issued guidance in August 2014 directing the SSAs, in coordination with their sector stakeholders, to update their sector-specific plans.[9] The SSAs are also to review and modify existing and future sector efforts to ensure that cyber concerns are fully integrated into sector security activities.

In addition, the NIPP sets up a framework for sharing information across and between federal and nonfederal stakeholders within each sector that includes the establishment of sector coordinating councils and government coordinating councils. Sector coordinating councils are to serve as a voice for the sector and a principal entry point for the government to collaborate with the sector for critical infrastructure security and resilience activities.[10] The government coordinating councils enable interagency, intergovernmental, and cross-jurisdictional coordination within and across sectors. Each government coordinating council is chaired by a representative from the designated SSA with responsibility for providing cross-sector coordination.[11]

The NIPP also recommended several activities—referred to as Call to Action steps— to guide the efforts of the SSAs and their sector partners to advance security and resilience under three broad activity categories: building on partnership efforts; innovating in risk management; and focusing on outcomes. Table 4 shows the 10 Call to Action Steps determined to have a cybersecurity-related nexus.[12]

Table 4. National Infrastructure Protection Plan Cybersecurity-Related Call to Action Steps

Build upon partnership efforts
• *Determine collective actions through planning efforts*—planning activities including updating the sector-specific plans that provide current and planned cybersecurity efforts.
• *Empower local and regional partnerships to build capacity nationally*—identifying local and regional collaborative partnerships to expand the reach of national preparedness activities including integrating human, physical, and cyber elements of critical infrastructure risk management.
• *Leverage incentives to advance security and resilience*[a]—encouraging investment in security and resilience measures with effortssuch as gathering data on the cost of the lack of security and establishing innovation challenge programs to spur new security solutions.
Innovate in managing risk:
• *Enable risk-informed decision making through enhanced situational awareness*[b]—improving practices for sharing information such as disseminating intelligence and information security products across sectors while protecting sensitive information.
• *Analyze infrastructure dependencies, interdependencies, and associated cascading effects*—mitigating the impact of incidents through an understanding of how sectors are dependent upon each other and upon information and communication technology.
• *Identify, assess, and respond to unanticipated infrastructure cascading effects during and following incidents*—developing and enhancing incident response capabilities in order to prioritize response and recovery efforts and minimize the consequences of anincident.
• *Strengthen coordinated development and delivery of technical assistance, training, and education*—developing technical assistance and training and leveraging educational activities from the Department of Homeland Security and other sector-specific agencies (SSA).
• *Improve critical infrastructure security and resilience by advancing research and development solutions*—promoting researchand development and facilitating investments in cybersecurity innovations that infrastructure security and resilience.
Focus on outcomes
• *Evaluate progress toward the achievement of goals*—identifying high-level outputs associated with national goals and priorities and conducting annual data calls for SSAs to provide input to the national report on the critical infrastructure.
• *Learn and adapt during and after exercises and incidents*—coordinating security incident response exercises informed by lessons learned from prior exercises and used to enhance technical assistance, training, and education programs.

Source: GAO analysis of the NIPP Call to Action Steps. | GAO-16-79

[a] According to Presidential Policy Directive 21, resilience is the ability to prepare for and adapt to changing conditions and withstand and recover rapidly from disruptions. It includes the ability to withstand and recover from deliberate attacks, accidents, or naturally occurring threats or incidents.

[b] The NIPP defines situational awareness as sharing information and applying the knowledge gained through changes in policy, process, and culture to be current with a dynamic and evolving risk environment.

The NIPP states that all of the identified steps, including these 10 actions with a greater relationship to enhancing cybersecurity, are not intended to be exhaustive or implemented in every sector. Rather, they are to provide strategic direction, allow for differing priorities in each sector, and enable continuous improvement of security and resilience efforts.

In addition, Executive Order 13636 was issued to, among other things, address the need to improve cybersecurity through information sharing and collaboratively developing and implementing risk-based standards.[13] It called for the SSAs to, among other things, establish, in coordination with DHS, a voluntary program to support the adoption of the National Institute of Standards and Technology's (NIST) Framework for Improving Critical Infrastructure Cybersecurity (Cybersecurity Framework)[14] by owners and operators of critical infrastructure and any other interested entities; create incentives to encourage owners and operators of critical infrastructure to participate in the voluntary program; and, if necessary, develop implementation guidance or supplemental materials to address sector-specific risks and operating environments.

SECTOR-SPECIFIC AGENCIES DETERMINED THAT CYBER RISKS WERE SIGNIFICANT FOR MOST SECTORS

Sector-specific agencies determined the significance of cyber risk to the networks and industrial control systems for all 15 of the sectors in the scope of our review. Specifically, they determined that cyber risk was significant for 11 of 15 sectors. For the remaining 4 sectors, the SSAs had determined that cyber risks were not significant due to the lack of cyber dependence in the sector's operations, among other reasons. These determinations were carried out in response to the 2009 NIPP, which directed the SSAs to consider how cyber would be prioritized among their sectors' critical infrastructure and key resources as part of the sector- specific planning process. The SSAs and their sector stakeholders were to include an overview of current and emerging sector risks including those affecting cyber when preparing their 2010 plans. Table 5 shows the significance of cyber risk to each sector, as determined by the SSAs, as well as when these determinations were made.

Table 5. Significance of Cyber Risk to Critical Infrastructure Sectors, as Determined by Sector-Specific Agencies' Most Current Documented Analysis

Sector	Sector-specific agency	Cyber risk significant to sector?	Year of risk determination
Chemical	Department of Homeland Security (DHS)	Yes	2010
Commercial Facilities	DHS	No	2010
Communications	DHS	Yes	2012
Critical Manufacturing	DHS	No	2010
Dams	DHS	No	2010
Defense Industrial Base	Department of Defense	Yes	2010
Emergency Services	DHS	Yes	2012
Energy	Department of Energy	Yes	2010
Financial Services	Department of the Treasury	Yes	2010
Food and Agriculture	U.S. Department of Agriculture, Department of Health and Human Services	No	2010
Health Care and Public Health	Department of Health and Human Services	Yes	2010
Information Technology	DHS	Yes	2009
Nuclear Reactors, Materials, and Waste	DHS	Yes	2010
Transportation Systems	DHS, Department of Transportation	Yes	2014
Water and Wastewater Systems	Environmental Protection Agency	Yes	2010

Source: GAO analysis of agency data. | GAO-16-79

Since most of these determinations were made for the 2010 sector-specific planning process, they may not reflect the current risk environment of the sectors. In particular, SSAs for the 4 sectors that had not determined cyber risks to be significant during their 2010 sector- specific planning process subsequently reconsidered the significance of cyber risks to their sectors. Also, in response to the 2013 NIPP, DHS issued guidance for developing updated sector-specific plans for 2015. According to this guidance and SSA officials, SSAs are to document how they have reconsidered the significance of cyber risks to their sectors. DHS officials stated that the SSAs have drafted their updated sector- specific plans and submitted them to DHS for review; however, the plans have not yet been finalized and released.

Based on the 2010 sector-specific plans and subsequent documents and activities, the SSAs' determinations of the significance of cyber risk to their 15 respective sectors are summarized below.

Chemical Sector

DHS, in collaboration with chemical sector stakeholders, determined that cyber risk was a significant priority for the sector. In 2009, DHS and the chemical sector coordinating council issued the Roadmap to Secure Controls Systems in the Chemical Sector,[15] which documented the cybersecurity concerns for chemical facilities' industrial control systems and the need to develop cyber risk mitigation actions to be addressed over a 10-year period. In addition, the 2010 Chemical Sector-Specific Plan[16] highlighted the importance of cyber systems to the sector and promoted the need for owners and operators of sector assets to apply risk assessment and management methodologies to identify cyber threats to their individual operations.

Commercial Facilities Sector

DHS did not consider cyber risks to be significant for the commercial facilities sector. The commercial facilities sector's 2010 sector-specific plan does not identify cyber risks as significant to the sector. DHS officials stated that the decision was based on the sector's diversity of components and the manner in which cyber-related technology is employed. According to these officials, a cyber event affecting one facility's cyber systems (e.g., access control or environmental systems) would not be likely to affect the cyber assets of other facilities within the sector.

However, in July 2015, DHS officials stated that, as part of the updated sector planning process, they had recognized cyber risk as a high-priority concern for the sector. In particular, they noted that the sector uses Internet-connected systems for processes like ticketing and reservations, so a large-scale communications failure or cyber attack could disrupt the sector's operations.

Communications Sector

DHS, in collaboration with communications sector stakeholders, completed a risk assessment in 2012 for the communications sector that identified cyber risk as a significant priority; however, the assessment noted that due to the sector's diversity and level of resiliency, most of the threats would only result in local or regional communications disruptions or outages.[17] The assessment evaluated cyber threats such as malicious and non-malicious actors committing alterations or intrusions that could pose local, regional, or national level risks to broadcasting, cable, satellite, wireless, and wireline communications networks. The risk assessment also concluded that malicious actors could use the communications sector to attack other sectors.

Critical Manufacturing Sector

DHS did not consider cyber risk to be significant for the critical manufacturing sector. The sector's 2010 sector-specific plan stated that many critical manufacturing owners and operators from this diverse and dispersed sector had completed asset, system, or network-specific assessments on their own initiative. Also, the plan identified cyber elements that support the sector's functional areas, including electronic systems for processing the information necessary for management and operation or for automatic control of physical processes in manufacturing. This applied primarily to the production of metals, machinery, electrical equipment, and heavy equipment. However, the critical manufacturing sector relies upon other sectors such as communications and information technology where addressing cyber risk is a priority.

DHS officials stated that, since 2010, they have identified sector critical cyber functions and services, and the sector's draft 2015 sector-specific plan notes this as a step toward conducting a sector-wide cyber risk assessment.

Dams Sector

DHS officials considered cyber risks for the dams sector and acknowledged that cyber threats could have negative consequences; however, they determined cyber risks to not be significant for the sector. Specifically, the sector's 2010 sector-specific plan concluded that the sector's cyber environment and its legacy industrial control systems were designed to operate in a fairly isolated environment using proprietary software, hardware, and communications technology and, as a result, were designed with cybersecurity as a low priority. However, the officials stated that vulnerabilities in industrial control systems pose cyber-related risks to the sector's operations. In the sector-specific plan, they acknowledged that the evolution of industrial control systems to incorporate network-based and Internet Protocol-addressable features and more commercially available technologies could introduce many of the same vulnerabilities that exist in current networked information systems.

DHS officials also stated that they are addressing cybersecurity for the sector with their update to the sector-specific plan and the sector's roadmap for securing control systems, as well as with the development of a capability maturity model specifically for the dams sector. At the time of our review, the updated sector-specific plan was still in draft.

Defense Industrial Base Sector

The Department of Defense (DOD) determined that cyber threats to contractors' unclassified information systems represented an unacceptable risk of compromise to DOD information and posed a significant risk to U.S. national security and economic security interests. In the sector's 2010 sector-specific plan, DOD, in collaboration with its sector partners, listed cybersecurity and managing risk to information among its five goals for the sector's protection and resilience. In addition, DOD has issued annual "for official use only" reports on its progress defending DOD and the defense industrial base against cyber events for fiscal years 2010 through 2014.[18] The reports identify definitions and categories of cyber events, exploited vulnerabilities, and adversary intrusion methods based on data from several key DOD organizations with cybersecurity responsibilities and other intelligence sources. The reports are to provide an annual update of cyber threats, threat sources, and vulnerability trends affecting the defense industrial base.

Emergency Services Sector

DHS officials, in collaboration with sector stakeholders, concluded that cyber threats could have a significant impact on the emergency services sector's operations. The risk assessment process brought together subject matter experts to perform an assessment of cyber risks across six emergency services sector disciplines: law enforcement, fire and emergency services, emergency medical services, emergency management, public works, and public safety communications and coordination/fusion. They developed cyber risk scenarios across multiple sector disciplines and applied DHS's Cybersecurity Assessment and Risk Management Approach methodology to reach their conclusion.[19] The results were reported in 2012 in the Emergency Services Sector Cyber Risk Assessment.[20]

In a previous GAO review of cybersecurity in the emergency services sector, we reported that sector planning activities, including the cyber risk assessment, did not address the more interconnected, Internet-based emerging technologies becoming more prevalent in the emergency services sector. As a result, the sector could be vulnerable to cyber risks in the future without more comprehensive planning.[21] We recommended that the Secretary of Homeland Security collaborate with emergency services sector stakeholders to address the cybersecurity implications of implementing technology initiatives in related plans. DHS agreed with our recommendation and stated that the updated sector-specific plan will include consideration of the sector's emerging technology. At the time of our review, the updated sector-specific plan was still in draft.

Energy Sector

The Department of Energy (DOE) identified cyber risks as significant and a priority for the energy sector. Specifically, in the sector's 2010 sector-specific plan, DOE, in collaboration with its sector stakeholders, included cybersecurity among the sector's goals to enhance preparedness, security, and resilience. DOE officials stressed that their risk management approach focuses on resilience, especially in the context of ensuring the resilience of the electric grid. In addition, the 2011 Roadmap to Achieve Energy Delivery System Cybersecurity, developed by energy sector stakeholders, including responsible DOE officials, recognized the continually evolving cyber threats and vulnerabilities and provided a framework for energy sector stakeholders to survive a cyber incident while sustaining critical functions.

Financial Services Sector

Treasury, in collaboration with sector stakeholders, identified cyber risk as significant to the financial services sector. Specifically, the 2010 financial services sector-specific plan stated that all of the sector's services rely on its cyber infrastructure, which necessitates that cybersecurity be factored into all of the sector's critical infrastructure protection activities. In addition, as a highly regulated sector, the financial services sector has been required to undergo risk assessments by financial regulators to satisfy regulatory requirements.

In July 2015, Treasury officials stated that they leveraged the collective body of risk assessment data to determine the sector's overall risk profile, which will be included in the 2015 sector-specific plan. At the time of our review, the updated sector-specific plan was still in draft.

Food and Agriculture Sector

The U.S. Department of Agriculture (USDA) and the Department of Health and Human Services' Food and Drug Administration (FDA), in collaboration with their sector stakeholders, determined that the significance of cyber risk was low for the food and agriculture sector when the SSP was developed in 2010. As stated in the plan, the sector did not perceive itself as a target of cyber attack and concluded that, based on the nature of its operations, a cyber attack would pose the risk of only minimal economic disruption. However, the plan acknowledged the rapidly evolving cyber environment and the need to revisit the issue in the future.

In July 2015, USDA officials stated that they had reconsidered the significance of cyber risk and the role of cybersecurity in the sector and that it would be reflected in the yet-to-be-released 2015 sector-specific plan. In addition, according to USDA officials, they had completed a sector risk assessment effort with assistance from DHS.

Health Care and Public Health Sector

The Department of Health and Human Services (HHS), in collaboration with its sector partners, identified cyber risk as significant to the health care and public health sector. Specifically, the 2010 sector-specific plan identified cybersecurity and mitigating risks to the sector's cyber assets as one of four service continuity goals for the sector. The plan's cybersecurity risk assessment section identified and categorized common cyber threats, vulnerabilities, consequences, and mitigation strategies for the sector. Also, HHS and its partners added cyber infrastructure protection as a research and development priority in the sector-specific plan. In addition, health care entities, such as health plans and providers that maintain health data, must assess risks to cyber-based systems based on Health Insurance Portability and Accountability Act of 1996 security requirements.[22]

Information Technology Sector

DHS, in collaboration with information technology sector stakeholders, identified cyber risk as a sector priority. DHS and its sector partners determined that the consequences of cyber incidents or events would be of great concern and would affect the sector's ability to produce or provide critical products and services. DHS worked with public and private information technology stakeholders to complete the Information Technology Sector Baseline Risk Assessment in 2009.[23] The risk assessment focused on risks to the processes involved in the creation of IT products and services and critical IT functions including research and development, manufacturing, distribution, upgrades, and maintenance— and not on specific organizations or assets.[24]

Nuclear Sector

DHS and its nuclear sector stakeholders prioritized cyber risk as a significant risk for the nuclear sector. According to the 2011 Roadmap to Enhance Cyber Systems Security in the Nuclear Sector,[25] they determined that the cyber systems supporting the nuclear sector are at risk due to the increasing volume, complexity, speed, and connectedness of the nuclear sector's systems. Therefore, DHS and its sector partners included protecting against the exploitation of the sector's cyber assets, systems, and networks among its sector goals and objectives for a comprehensive protective posture.

Transportation Systems Sector

Addressing cyber risk is a significant priority for the transportation systems sector. In the 2010 transportation systems sector-specific plan, DHS's Transportation Security Administration (TSA) and U.S. Coast Guard[26] acknowledged the importance of cyber assets to the sector's operations across the various transportation modes and included an overview of the risk management framework, an all-hazards approach to be applied to the physical, human, and cyber components of the infrastructure. They also established goals and objectives to shape their sector partners' approach for managing sector risk. As part of their objective to enhance the all-hazard preparedness and resilience of the transportation systems sector, they included the need to identify critical cyber assets, systems, and networks and implement measures to address strategic cybersecurity priorities.

For fiscal year 2014, TSA assessed risks to the transportation systems sector and reported the outcome to Congress.[27] Although the assessment did not specifically quantify cyber risks for the sector, it considered cyber threats to transportation modes in hypothetical scenarios, such as the effect of a cyber attack disabling a public transit system. In addition, TSA's Office of Intelligence and Analysis provides transportation mode-specific annual threat assessments that include malicious cyber activity as part of the analysis. For example, the pipeline modal threat assessment considered computer network attacks that could disrupt pipeline functions and computer network exploitations that could allow unauthorized network access and theft of information. In addition, we have previously reported that the Coast Guard needs to address cybersecurity in the maritime port environment by, among other things, including cyber risks in its biennial maritime risk assessment.[28]

Subsequently, the Coast Guard released its updated risk assessment for maritime operations, which identified the need to address cyber risk but did not identify vulnerabilities in relevant cyber assets.[29]

Water and Wastewater Systems (Water) Sector

The Environmental Protection Agency (EPA), in collaboration with sector partners, determined that a cyber attack is a significant risk to the water sector. Cyber attacks on the industrial control systems are among the plausible hazards that threaten the water and wastewater systems sector, according to the risk assessment portion of the 2010 sector-specific plan. EPA concluded that attacks on the systems used to monitor and control water movement and treatment could disrupt operations at water and wastewater facilities, although the capability to employ manual overrides for critical systems could reduce the consequences of an attack. EPA recommended that water sector facilities regularly update or conduct an all-hazards risk assessment that includes cyber attacks as a priority threat. Further, the Roadmap to a Secure and Resilient Water Sector,[30] developed in 2013 by EPA, DHS, and water sector partners, included advancing the development of sector-specific cybersecurity resources as a top priority for the sector.

Sector-Specific Agencies Generally Performed Cyber Risk Mitigation Activities

Sector-specific agencies generally took actions to mitigate cyber risks and vulnerabilities for their respective sectors that address the Call to Action steps in the National Infrastructure Protection Plan. While the steps are not required of the SSAs, they are intended to guide national progress while allowing for differing priorities in different sectors. The SSAs had taken action to address most of the nine NIPP Call to Action steps.[31] While SSAs for 12 of the 15 sectors had not identified incentives to promote cybersecurity in their sectors, as called for by one of the Call to Action steps, all the SSAs have participated in a working group to identify appropriate incentives to encourage cybersecurity improvements across their respective sectors. In addition, SSAs for 3 of 15 sectors had not yet made significant progress in advancing cyber-based research and development within their sectors because it had not been an area of focus for their sector. DHS guidance for updating the sector-specific plans directs the SSAs to incorporate the NIPP's actions to guide their cyber risk mitigation activities including cybersecurity-related actions to identify incentives and promote research and development.

Figure 1 depicts NIPP Call to Action steps addressed by SSAs. (App. II provides further details on actions taken to address the Call to Action steps for each sector.)

Chemical Sector

DHS implemented activities to mitigate the cyber risks for the chemical sector for eight of nine of the NIPP's Call to Action steps; however, it had not established incentives to encourage its sector partners to voluntarily invest in cybersecurity-enhancing measures. DHS has developed technical resources, cybersecurity awareness tools, and information- sharing mechanisms among its activities to enhance the sector's cybersecurity. DHS officials described other cybersecurity activities in development including updates to sector cybersecurity guidance that could include incentives; however, they were unable to identify specific incentives to encourage cybersecurity across the sector.

Commercial Facilities Sector

DHS conducted cyber mitigation activities that aligned with eight of the nine NIPP Call to Action steps for the commercial facilities sector. DHS provided technical assistance and supported information-sharing efforts for the sector. For example, it developed a risk self-assessment tool in conjunction with sector partners to raise awareness of the importance of their cyber systems. DHS also promoted a number of information-sharing mechanisms available through its Office of Cybersecurity and Communications, including the dissemination of alerts through the U.S. Computer Emergency Readiness Team (US-CERT), ICS-CERT, and the Commercial Facilities Cyber Working Group, among others. However, DHS did not identify efforts to establish incentives to encourage commercial facilities sector partners to implement cybersecurity- enhancing measures.

Call to Action Steps	Chemical	Commercial facilities	Communications	Critical manufacturing	Dams	Defense industrial base	Emergency services	Energy	Financial services	Food and agriculture	Healthcare and public health	Information technology	Nuclear reactors, materials, and waste	Transportation systems	Water and wastewater systems
Determine collective actions through joint planning efforts	●	●	●	●	●	●	●	●	●	●	●	●	●	●	●
Empower local and regional partnerships to build capacity nationally	●	●	●	●	●	●	●	●	●	●	●	○	●	●	●
Leverage incentives to advance security and resilience	○	○	○	○	○	○	○	●	○	○	●	○	○	●	○
Enable risk-informed decision making through enhanced situational awareness	●	●	●	●	●	●	●	●	●	●	●	●	●	●	●
Analyze infrastructure dependencies, interdependencies, and associated cascading effects	●	●	●	●	●	●	●	●	●	●	●	●	●	●	●
Identify, assess, and respond to unanticipated infrastructure cascading effects during and following incidents	●	●	●	●	●	●	●	●	●	●	●	●	●	●	●
Strengthen coordinated development and delivery of technical assistance, training, and education	●	●	●	●	●	●	●	●	●	●	●	●	●	●	●
Improve critical infrastructure security and resilience by advancing research and development solutions	●	●	●	○	●	●	●	●	●	○	○	●	●	●	●
Learn and adapt during and after exercises and incidents	●	●	●	●	●	●	●	●	●	○	●	●	●	●	●

● Steps were addressed ○ Steps were **NOT** addressed

Source: GAO analysis of agency documentation. | GAO-16-79

Figure 1. Call to Action Steps Addressed by Sector-Specific Agencies for Each Sector.

Communications Sector

DHS worked to reduce risk to the communications sector through collaborative cyber risk mitigation activities that align with eight of nine NIPP Call to Action steps. However, DHS did not establish incentives to promote cybersecurity for the sector. As previously stated, DHS and its communications sector partners completed the 2012 National Sector Risk Assessment for Communications, which examined risks from cyber incidents or events that threaten the sector's cyber assets, systems, and networks. According to DHS officials, it coordinated mitigation activities with its communications sector partners and addressed risks identified through the assessment process. In addition, officials explained that it implemented or facilitated sector-wide information-sharing mechanisms with such entities as the National Cybersecurity and Communications Integration Center, National

Infrastructure Coordinating Center, and National Coordinating Center for Telecommunications and Communications Information Sharing and Analysis Center.

Although DHS had not implemented specific cyber-related incentives for the communications sector, DHS officials stated that National Security staff and the Office of Policy have been working on possible national incentives such as tax credits for future use.

Critical Manufacturing Sector

DHS focused cyber risk mitigation activities in seven of nine NIPP Call to Action steps for the critical manufacturing sector. However, cyber risk mitigation activities did not include efforts to incentivize cybersecurity or support cybersecurity-related research and development. Among its cyber risk mitigation activities, DHS participated in information sharing efforts through the sector coordinating council to enhance situational awareness; and led outreach efforts to encourage diverse (i.e., small, medium, and large companies) participation in the council as an activity to build national capacity.

Although specific incentives to encourage cybersecurity across the sector had not been put in place, DHS officials stated that they had been involved in a working group to study possible options such as cyber insurance. While the critical manufacturing sector-specific plan and associated annual report of sector activities indicated that goals and needs regarding sector research and development are areas for future development, DHS did not provide any examples of specific research and development activities addressing the sector's cybersecurity.

Dams Sector

DHS developed cyber risk mitigation activities for the dams sector focused on eight of nine NIPP Call to Action steps. However, DHS did not identify activities leveraging incentives to advance security and resilience. DHS officials stated that their efforts had not focused on incentives. Among its cyber risk mitigation activities, DHS officials facilitated the development of the Dams Sector Roadmap to Secure Control Systems, developed in 2010, which focuses on the cybersecurity of industrial control systems where cyber risks maybe more significant for individual entities. DHS also supported information-sharing mechanisms by promoting sector-wide information sharing and organized a cybersecurity working group to discuss cyber-relevant topics during quarterly meetings. Further, the department disseminated cyber vulnerability information to sector partners through advisories and alerts from DHS's ICS-CERT and US-CERT.

Defense Industrial Base Sector

DOD devised cyber risk mitigation activities that align with eight of nine NIPP Call to Action steps but had not established incentives to promote cybersecurity. Cyber risk mitigation activities included sharing threat information and mitigation strategies for enhanced situational awareness and participating in DOD-centric exercises, among others.

Although DOD did not identify specific incentives to encourage cybersecurity in the defense industrial base sector, DOD officials stated that they joined an interagency effort to explore various incentives that might be offered to industry to encourage use of the NIST Cybersecurity Framework.

In addition, DOD officials noted that they have worked with the General Services Administration to develop strategic guidelines to incorporate cybersecurity standards in requirements for DOD contractors; however, this effort would not be part of DOD's voluntary sector cybersecurity program.[32]

Emergency Services Sector

DHS established or facilitated cyber risk mitigation activities for eight of nine NIPP Call to Action steps; however, it had not instituted cybersecurity incentives. DHS officials stated that grants to state and local governments as incentives to encourage cybersecurity were not available, and no other types of incentives were identified. Among its activities, the department collaborated with emergency services sector partners in March 2014 to develop the Emergency Services Sector Roadmap to Secure Voice and Data Systems, which identified and discussed proposed risk mitigation activities and included justification for the response, sector context, barriers to implementation, and suggestions for implementation.[33] DHS officials also noted various information-sharing mechanisms that disseminate cyber threat and vulnerability information to sector partners and allow reporting back to DHS.

Energy Sector

DOE instituted or supported cyber risk mitigation activities that correspond to all nine of the NIPP Call to Action steps. For example, DOE provided grants to share the costs of sector partners' cybersecurity innovation efforts as an incentive for advancing cybersecurity and to support research and development of solutions to improve critical infrastructure security and resilience. Other activities to encourage cybersecurity in the sector included the development of cybersecurity guidance to promote the use of NIST's Cybersecurity Framework and establishing or supporting cyber threat information sharing mechanisms. DOE also developed and implemented the Cybersecurity Risk Information Sharing Program, a public-private partnership to facilitate the timely sharing of cyber threat information and develop situational awareness tools to enhance electric utility companies' ability to identify, prioritize, and coordinate the protection of their critical infrastructure.

Financial Services Sector

The Department of the Treasury implemented or facilitated activities that served to mitigate cyber risk for the financial services sector. These activities correspond to eight of the nine NIPP Call to Action steps. However, Treasury had not developed incentives to encourage cybersecurity in the sector through its voluntary critical infrastructure protection program. Treasury officials noted that they foresee developing incentives as a result of a report to the President pursuant to an Executive Order 13636 requirement that outlined an approach for policymakers to evaluate the benefits and relative effectiveness of government incentives in promoting adoption of NIST's Cybersecurity Framework.[34] Using the results of the updated sector planning process to inform its efforts could assist Treasury in developing any such incentives, as appropriate.

We have previously reported on additional efforts to address cyber risk in this sector. In July 2015, we reported on cyber attacks against depository institutions, banking regulators' oversight of cyber risk mitigation activities, and the process for sharing cyber threat information.[35] Specifically, we found that smaller depository institutions were greater targets for cyber attacks. Also, we noted that although financial regulators devoted considerable resources to overseeing information security at larger institutions, their limited IT staff resources generally meant that examiners with little or no IT expertise were performing IT examinations at smaller institutions. As a result, we recommended that these regulators collect and analyze additional trend information that could further increase their ability to identify patterns in problems across institutions and better target their reviews. Finally, with cyber threat information coming from multiple sources, including from Treasury and other federal entities, recipients contacted in the review found federal information repetitive, not always timely, and not always readily usable. To help address these needs, Treasury had various efforts under way to obtain such information and confidentially share it with other institutions, including participating in groups that monitor and provide threat information on cyber incidents.

Food and Agriculture Sector

USDA and FDA, as co-SSAs for the food and agriculture sector, had cyber risk mitigation activities addressing six of the nine NIPP Call to Action steps. For example, the SSAs had encouraged sector-wide participation in DHS's program to promote NIST's Cybersecurity Framework, participated in the process to identify any cyber-dependent critical functions and services, and supported threat briefings to enhance situational awareness across the sector. According to food and agriculture SSA officials, they had other activities in progress including facilitated sessions with their sector stakeholders as part of assessing risks to the sector and considering the development of food and agriculture sector-specific NIST Cybersecurity Framework implementation guidance to make the framework more relatable to food and agriculture stakeholders.

However, other areas, including incentives to promote cybersecurity, research and development of security and resilience solutions, and lessons learned from exercises and incidents, have yet to be developed. As stated earlier, during the 2010 sector-specific planning process, cybersecurity risk was not considered significant for the sector, but USDA and FDA officials stated that they had incorporated cyber risk into their updated sector-specific plan and they continue to develop cybersecurity- related activities for the sector.

Health Care and Public Health Sector

HHS developed or supported activities addressing eight of the nine NIPP Call to Action steps. For example, HHS leveraged the private sector clearance program and access to classified information as incentives for sector stakeholders to participate in cybersecurity-enhancing activities. However, HHS had not performed any activities related to cybersecurity research and development. HHS officials stated that promoting research and development efforts to enhance the sector's cybersecurity was not a focus of their cyber risk mitigation activities during fiscal years 2014 and 2015.

Information Technology Sector

DHS, in collaboration with its information technology sector partners, implemented risk mitigation activities to enhance the sector's cybersecurity environment. We identified activities that addressed eight of nine NIPP Call to Action steps. DHS's IT sector cyber risk mitigation activities included the promotion of incident response and recovery capabilities, support for various cyber-related information sharing mechanisms, and capabilities for technical assistance to sector entities. However, DHS had not specifically identified and analyzed incentives to improve cybersecurity within the IT sector. DHS officials stated that they have collaborated with other federal agencies to develop options for cybersecurity enhancement incentives for the sector.

Nuclear Reactors, Materials, and Waste (Nuclear) Sector

DHS carried out risk mitigation activities that addressed eight of the nine NIPP Call to Action steps. These activities included collaborative efforts through established working groups and councils to share information about cybersecurity-related alerts, advisories, and strategies. DHS officials responsible for nuclear SSA efforts referred to the Roadmap to Enhance Cyber Systems Security in the Nuclear Sector as guidance they developed in June 2011 and disseminated to sector partners for determining cyber risk and a vision for mitigating it over a 15-year period.[36] However, DHS's cyber risk mitigation activities did not include incentives for nuclear sector partners to enhance cybersecurity.

Transportation Systems Sector

The Department of Transportation and DHS's TSA and U.S. Coast Guard put in place cyber risk mitigation activities in line with all nine NIPP Call to Action steps. For example, TSA shared cyber threat intelligence and information from the National Cybersecurity and Communications Integration Center to multiple transportation modes through its threat dissemination channels. In addition, classified information had been "tearlined" or downgraded based on a request from TSA so that information could be shared without sharing sensitive and restricted information to sector officials without security clearances.[37] Further, the U.S. Coast Guard used its Port Security Grant Program as an incentive for cybersecurity efforts through its Port Security Grants Program for the maritime subsector. This DHS grants program provides funding for maritime transportation security measures including cybersecurity. However, as we have previously reported, this program did not always make use of cybersecurity-related expertise and other information in allocating grants.[38] Accordingly, we recommended that the program take steps to make better-informed funding decisions. In addition, TSA officials stated that they have participated in working groups to identify other cybersecurity-related incentives across the various transportation modes.

Water Sector

EPA incorporated cyber risk mitigation activities that aligned with eight of the nine NIPP Call to Action steps. Specifically, EPA had not established incentives to encourage sector partners to enhance their security and resiliency. EPA officials stated providing funds to support cybersecurity enhancements would be an incentive for their sector partners; however, they lacked the resources to offer grants to implement security measures. EPA officials also stated that they are working on implementing recommendations from Critical Infrastructure Partnership Advisory Council Water Sector Cybersecurity Strategy Workgroup which include exploring ways to demonstrate how the benefits of implementing cybersecurity enhancements outweigh the costs of cyber incidents as an incentive to encourage investment in cybersecurity improvements.

Sector-Specific Agencies Collaborated across Sectors to Improve Cybersecurity Efforts

Sector-specific agencies use various collaborative mechanisms to share cybersecurity related information across all of the sectors. Presidential Policy Directive 21 (PPD-21) states that sector-specific agencies are to coordinate with DHS and other relevant federal departments and agencies and collaborate with critical infrastructure owners and operators to strengthen the security and resiliency of the nation's critical infrastructure.

Table 6. Information-Sharing Mechanisms Used by Sector-Specific Agencies

Organization	Description	Number of sectors represented
Federal Senior Leadership Council (FSLC)	The FSLC is composed of senior officials from the designated sector-specific agencies and other federal departments and agencies identified in PPD-21. The council facilitates enhanced federal communication and coordination across the sectors focused on critical infrastructure security and resilience.	15
government coordinating councils (GCCs)	GCCs are formed to enable interagency and cross-jurisdictional coordination. The GCCs are comprised of representatives from across various levels of government (federal, state, local, tribal or territorial), as appropriate to the operating landscape of each individual sector.	15
Critical Infrastructure Partnership Advisory Council (CIPAC)	The CIPAC convenes critical infrastructure owners, operators, and trade association members of sector coordinating councils (SCCs) and members of government coordinating councils (GCCs) to engage in intra-government and public-private cooperation, information sharing, and collaboration across the entire range of critical infrastructure protection activities.	15
Cross-Sector Cyber Security Working Group (CSCSWG)	The CSCSWG operates under the DHS Stakeholder Engagement and Cyber Infrastructure Resilience division and it enhances cybersecurity protection efforts by identifying opportunities to improve cross-sector cybersecurity coordination; highlighting cyber dependencies and interdependencies; identifying incentives to encourage cyber risk mitigation, and sharing cybersecurity products and findings.	14

Organization	Description	Number of sectors represented
Industrial Control Systems Joint Working Group (ICSJWG)	The ICSJWG is a collaborative and coordinating body formed under the Critical Infrastructure Partnership Advisory Council Framework. The ICSJWG facilitates partnerships between the federal government and private sector owners and operators in all critical infrastructure sectors.	12
National Cybersecurity and Communications Integration Center (NCCIC)	The NCCIC is a 24x7 cyber situational awareness, incident response, and management center that is a national nexus of cyber and communications integration for the federal government, intelligence community, and law enforcement. The NCCIC shares physical and cyber information and is co-located with the National Infrastructure Coordinating Center.	12
National Infrastructure Coordinating Center (NICC)	The NICC is a dedicated 24/7 coordination and information sharing operations center that maintains situational awareness of the nation's critical infrastructure for the federal government. The NICC shares physical and cyber information and is co-located with the NCCIC	12
Office of Cyber and Infrastructure Analysis (OCIA)	OCIA evaluates potential consequences of disruption from cyber threats and incidents to inform decisions to strengthen infrastructure security and resilience during incidents. OCIA works to advance understanding of emerging risks cross the cyber-physical domain. OCIA represents an integration and enhancement of DHS's analytic capabilities, supporting stakeholders and interagency partners.	13

Source: GAO analysis of agency-provided information. | GAO-16-79

SSAs share information and collaborate across sectors primarily through a number of councils, working groups, and information-sharing centers established by federal entities. The mechanisms identified during our review for SSAs to collaborate across the sectors are summarized, along with the number of sectors represented in each council or group by their respective SSA, in table 6.

The mechanisms provide SSAs opportunities to interact, collaborate, and coordinate with one another. For example, each of the sectors we reviewed used working groups created under the Critical Infrastructure Partnership Advisory Council. According to the CIPAC 2013 annual report, in 2012 there were 60 working groups that held approximately 200 meetings with objectives such as information sharing, training and exercises, and risk management.

In addition, SSAs used their respective government coordinating councils to coordinate with other SSAs about interdependencies and to gain access to needed expertise about the operations of other sectors. For example, DHS officials stated that the communications sector's government coordinating council membership provides the expertise necessary to fulfill the council's mission. They stated that its current membership includes representatives from the DOD, DOE and Treasury, among others, and from multiple DHS components.

Further, SSAs continually referred to the Cross-Sector Cyber Security Working Group and the Industrial Control System Joint Working Group as two of the main cybersecurity-related collaborative opportunities for federal agencies. Both of these working groups facilitate government sharing of information among officials representing different sectors. The Cross-Sector Cyber Security Working Group operates under DHS's Office of Cybersecurity and Communications. It provides the SSAs the opportunity to establish and maintain cross-sector partnerships; work on cross-cutting issues, such as incentives to encourage cybersecurity actions; and identify cyber dependencies and interdependencies that allow them to share information on cybersecurity trends that can affect their respective sectors. According to DHS, more than 100 members attend monthly meetings to share information and activities about their respective sectors. Of the SSAs representing the 15 sectors we reviewed, SSAs for 14 sectors indicated in their documentation or statements that they were active participants in this working group.

The Industrial Control System Joint Working Group was established by DHS's Industrial Control Systems Cyber Emergency Response Team to facilitate information sharing and reduce the risk to the nation's industrial control systems. According to DHS, the goal of this working group is to continue and enhance the collaborative efforts of the industrial control systems stakeholder community by accelerating the design, development, and deployment of secure industrial control systems. SSAs for 12 of the 15 sectors within the scope of our review were active participants in the working group. For example, HHS officials stated that they attend the Industrial Control System Joint Working Group meetings as a way to analyze relationships and identify overlapping actions with other sectors.

Table 7 provides examples of cross-sector collaboration in relation to the sectors.

Table 7. Examples of Sector-Specific Agencies' (SSA) Cross-Sector Collaborative Activities

Sector/SSA	Cross-sector collaboration activities
Chemical/Department of Homeland Security (DHS)	• Participated in the Cross-Sector Cyber Security Working Group (CSCSWG) and Industrial Control Systems Joint Working Group to address cybersecurity challenges through exchange of cross-sector perspectives and to discuss and address cybersecurity issues that impact industrial control systems. • Participated on the Federal Senior Leadership Council (FSLC), which was established to address common issues among the sectors, operational planning, and incident management. • Sponsored various information-sharing mechanisms including monthly suspicious/threat activity teleconferences, the Homeland Security Information Network-Critical Sectors, the Department of Homeland Security's Office of Cybersecurity and Communications Spotlight publication, and quarterly meetings with the sector coordinating council.
Commercial facilities/DHS	• Promoted a number of information-sharing mechanisms available through DHS's Office of Cybersecurity and Communications including the dissemination of alerts and cybersecurity best practices through the U.S. Computer Emergency Readiness Team (US-CERT), Industrial Control System Cyber Emergency Response Team (ICS-CERT), and the Commercial Facilities Cyber Working Group among others.
Communications/DHS	• Collaborated across sectors to improve cybersecurity postures, including through the Communications Sector Outreach and Awareness Webinar Series; Communications Security, Reliability, and Interoperability Council's Best Practices Working Group activities; participation in Federal Senior Leadership Council meetings; and Cross-Sector Cybersecurity Working Group by attending meetings and contributing to various products.
Critical manufacturing/DHS	• Participated in the CSCSWG.
Dams/DHS	• Participated in the CSCSWG.
Defense industrial base/Department of Defense	• Participated in the CSCSWG and FSLC.
Emergency services/DHS	• Leveraged the CSCSWG to promote cybersecurity information sharing among the SSAs.

Table 7. (Continued)

Sector/SSA	Cross-sector collaboration activities
Energy/Department of Energy	• Participated in the CSCSWG. • Participated in the Networking Information Technology Research and Development Program, which included research and development coordination topics such as cross-sector cybersecurity interdependencies.
Financial services/Department of the Treasury	• Worked collaboratively with Financial and Banking Information Infrastructure Committee members to address sector challenges, such as identifying metrics to evaluate progress and with the Department of Energy Communications Security, Reliability, and Interoperability Council because of the sector's dependence on the energy sector. • Participated in the FSLC for cross-sector collaboration efforts.
Food and agriculture/U.S. Department of Agriculture, Department of Health and Human Services (HHS)	• Participated in the CSCSWG and FSLC.
Health care and public health/HHS	• Participated in the Industrial Control Systems Joint Working Group and FSLC.
Information technology/DHS	• Participated, along with their sector partners, in cross-sector policy forums, including the Partnership for Critical Infrastructure Security, CSCSWG, Industrial Control Systems Joint Working Group, and Network Security Information Exchange. • Participated in the quarterly meetings of the FSLC.
Nuclear reactors, materials, and waste/DHS	• Facilitated collaboration between the Nuclear Sector Joint Cyber Sub council and DHS's Office of Cybersecurity and Communications to add more context to alerts andadvisories provided by entities such as US-CERT so that the sector stakeholders can quickly determine applicability and develop appropriate mitigation strategies.
Transportation systems/DHS, Department of Transportation	• Used coordination mechanisms to exchange information on its cybersecurity initiatives, including the CSCSWG and Industrial Control Systems Joint Working Group.
Water and wastewater systems/Environmental Protection Agency	• Engaged with the CSCSWG and the Industrial Control Systems Joint Working Group to enhance identification of cyber interdependencies between sectors.

Source: GAO analysis of SSA documentation. | GAO-16-79

In addition to the mechanisms identified above, further collaboration occurred through the co-location of sectors' SSAs within one department. DHS, as the SSA for eight critical infrastructure sectors, has six of the sectors assigned to officials under the Infrastructure Protection group, and two under the Cybersecurity and Communications group. DHS's Office of Infrastructure Protection officials representing several SSAs stated that they leverage DHS's Office of Cybersecurity and Communications capabilities and resources for their sectors. Further, housing these responsibilities within the same organization provided efficiencies for their respective critical infrastructure sectors. For example, according to documentation for the critical manufacturing sector SSA, officials are leveraging training curricula produced by other Office of Infrastructure Protection SSA officials. Additionally, DHS had co-located both the National Cybersecurity and Communications Integration Center and National Infrastructure Coordinating Center, which brings two 24x7 watch centers together as they share physical and cyber information related to critical infrastructure.

Finally, SSAs used the Homeland Information Sharing Network (HSIN) sector pages to collaborate across sectors. The HSIN is a network for homeland security mission operations to share sensitive but unclassified information, including with the critical infrastructure community. It is to provide real-time collaboration tools including a virtual meeting space, document sharing, alerts, and instant messaging. Officials from SSAs associated with 14 of the 15 sectors stated that they used HSIN to share information with stakeholders within their respective sectors. For example, within the dams HSIN portal, the sector implemented a Suspicious Activity Report online tool to provide users with the capability to report and retrieve information pertaining to suspicious activities that could compromise the facility or system in a manner that would cause an incident jeopardizing life or property. Additionally, officials from the chemical sector stated that they use HSIN for the coordination of cybersecurity incidents within the sector and officials from the critical manufacturing SSA stated that when entities from their sector reach out to them for more information on threats or alerts, they direct them to subscribe to the critical manufacturing HSIN page.

Most SSAs have not Developed Performance Measures to Monitor Sectors' Progress toward Improving Cybersecurity

The NIPP includes guidance to SSAs to focus on the outcomes of their security and resilience activities. Specifically, as noted earlier, one of the NIPP Call to Action steps directs SSAs and their sector partners to identify high-level outcomes to facilitate evaluation of progress toward national goals and priorities, including securing critical infrastructure against cyber threats. In addition, the NIPP risk management framework, used as a basis for the sector-specific plans, includes measuring the effectiveness of the SSAs' risk mitigation activities as a method of monitoring sector progress.

Among the SSAs, DOD, DOE, and HHS had established performance metrics to monitor cybersecurity-related activities, incidents, and progress in their sectors.

- DOD monitored cybersecurity for the defense industrial base sector through reports of cyber incidents and cyber incidents that were blocked; reports from owners and operators regarding efforts to execute the sector-specific plan's implementation actions; and the number of cyber threat products disseminated by DOD to cleared companies and the timeliness of shared threat information. DOD also prepared annual reports for Congress for fiscal years 2010 through 2014 that provided information on sector performance metrics.
- DOE developed the ieRoadmap, an interactive tool designed to enable energy sector stakeholders to map their energy delivery system cybersecurity efforts to specific milestones identified in the Roadmap to Achieve Energy Delivery Systems Cybersecurity. DOE also established the Cybersecurity Capability Maturity Model program to support ongoing development and measurement of cybersecurity capabilities. The voluntary program provides a mechanism for measuring cybersecurity capabilities from a management and program perspective.
- HHS monitored cybersecurity metrics such as the number of subscribers to receive its security alerts and incidents of health information security breaches. The Health Information Technology for Economic and Clinical Health (HITECH) Act[39] requires that health care data breaches be reported to the affected individuals and

HHS, compiled in an annual HHS report to Congress, and for breaches affecting 500 or more individuals, shared with the media. HHS officials stated that they use the information on data breaches as an indicator of cybersecurity-related trends for the sector.

However, SSAs for the other 12 sectors had not developed or reported performance metrics, although some had efforts under way to do so. For selected sectors, including financial services and water and wastewater systems, SSAs emphasized that they rely on their private sector partners to voluntarily share information and so are challenged in gathering the information needed to measure efforts. Sector stakeholders are not necessarily willing to openly share potentially sensitive cybersecurity- related information. Also, the DHS guidance to the SSAs for updating their sector-specific plans includes directions to create new metrics to evaluate the sectors' security and resilience progress; however, the plans have not been finalized and released.

DHS had not developed performance metrics to monitor the cybersecurity progress for its 8 sectors, although according to agency officials, such efforts are under way. For example, DHS lacked metrics for the chemical sector; however, officials stated that multiple industry working groups were working on cyber performance metrics to measure progress at a very high level. In addition, in 2011, a nuclear cybersecurity roadmap document was released that outlined milestones and specific cybersecurity goals for the sector over a 15-year period, including the need for metrics to measure and assess the sector's cybersecurity posture. The nuclear sector roadmap provides near-, mid-, and long-term goals but not specific measures or criteria to assess the sector's cybersecurity posture.

Further, according to DHS officials, a number of initiatives were begun to gather performance-related information, including the following:

- DHS's Programmatic Planning and Metrics Initiative was established in October 2014 to gather data from the department's sectors and monitor their cybersecurity process. However, as of the time of our review, the initiative had only limited historical data.
- DHS's Sector Outreach and Programs Division plans to implement program metrics to measure and analyze adoption of cybersecurity practices and NIST's Cybersecurity Framework across the sectors.[40]
- DHS officials for the information technology and communications sectors stated that they had proposed performance metrics to be implemented through 2018. In a review of cybersecurity related to the

nation's communications networks, we reported that DHS and its partners had not developed outcome-based metrics related to the cyber-protection activities for the communications sector.[41] We recommended that DHS and its sector partners develop, implement, and track sector outcome-oriented performance measures for cyber protection activities related to the nation's communications networks.

Regarding the financial services sector, Treasury officials stated that the department does not have performance metrics to chart the sector's cybersecurity-related progress. However, according to Treasury officials, the sector coordinating council is working with the Financial and Banking Information Infrastructure Committee[42] to identify metrics to evaluate progress in the sector. According to the officials, identifying actionable metrics based on cyber risk mitigation programs is a challenge. Treasury officials emphasized that the information needed is privately owned and may or may not be voluntarily shared with government partners.

The food and agriculture 2010 sector-specific plan stated that the sector did not have metrics to measure the effectiveness of risk mitigation efforts, although it acknowledged the need to establish tracking and monitoring mechanisms. The plan also noted that sector partners, including state agencies and private industry, may view reporting programmatic data as a burden and question the security of the data once reported. In December 2014, USDA officials noted that they do not have formal mechanisms to measure sector progress, although survey results collected through food safety inspection activities have some security elements. The ongoing process to update the sector-specific plan provides USDA and HHS an opportunity to consider possible performance metrics for monitoring the sector's cybersecurity progress.

The transportations systems sector SSAs had also not instituted mechanisms to evaluate the progress of sector entities in achieving a more secure sector. For example, TSA officials stated that they are developing cyber metrics in line with the 2014 Sector-Specific Plan Guidance; however, the officials noted that their industry partners are reluctant to share information needed to monitor improvement in the sector because they fear regulation.

Finally, EPA does not collect performance information to provide metrics on the effectiveness of its cybersecurity programs for the water sector. Agency officials noted that the lack of statutory authority is a major challenge to collecting performance metrics data. In the absence of statutory authority or agency policy, EPA must work with water sector associations to collect the information across the sector. However, water utilities may be reluctant to voluntarily report security information to EPA. EPA is also working with the Water Sector Coordinating Council to identify performance metrics for implementation of NIST's Cybersecurity Framework in the water sector, according to agency officials.

Until SSAs develop performance metrics and collect data to report on the progress of the sector-specific agencies' efforts to enhance the sectors' cybersecurity posture, they may be unable to adequately monitor the effectiveness of their cyber risk mitigation activities and document the resulting sector-wide cybersecurity progress.

CONCLUSIONS

Overall, SSAs are acting to address sector cyber risk, but additional monitoring actions could enhance their respective sectors' cybersecurity posture. Most SSAs had identified the significance of cyber risk to their respective sectors as part of the 2010 sector-specific planning process with four sectors concluding that cyber risk was not significant at that time, but subsequently reconsidering the significance of cyber risks to their sectors. However, to prepare the 2015 updates to their sector- specific plans, the planning guidance directed the SSAs to address their current and emerging sector risks including the cyber risk landscape and key trends shaping their approach to managing risk. Toward this end, all of the SSAs had generally performed cyber risk mitigation activities that address the NIPP's Call to Actions steps and regarding incentives— one area not addressed by most of the SSAS— efforts had begun to determine appropriate ways to encourage additional cybersecurity-related efforts across the nation's critical infrastructures.

To their credit, SSAs are engaged in multiple public-private and cross sector collaboration mechanisms that facilitate the sharing of information, including cybersecurity-related information. However, most SSAs have not developed metrics to measure and improve the effectiveness of all their cyber risk mitigation activities and their sectors' cybersecurity posture. As a result, SSAs may not be able to adequately monitor and document the benefits of their activities in improving the sectors' cybersecurity posture or determine how those efforts could be improved.

Recommendations for Executive Action

To better monitor and provide a basis for improving the effectiveness of cybersecurity risk mitigation activities, we recommend that, informed by the sectors' updated plans and in collaboration with sector stakeholders, the

- Secretary of Homeland Security direct responsible officials to develop performance metrics to provide data and determine how to overcome challenges to monitoring the chemical, commercial facilities, communications, critical manufacturing, dams, emergency services, information technology, and nuclear sectors' cybersecurity progress;
- Secretary of the Treasury direct responsible officials to develop performance metrics to provide data and determine how to overcome challenges to monitoring the financial services sector's cybersecurity progress;
- Secretaries of Agriculture and Health and Human Services (as co-SSAs) direct responsible officials to develop performance metrics to provide data and determine how to overcome challenges to monitoring the food and agriculture sector's cybersecurity progress;
- Secretaries of Homeland Security and Transportation (as co-SSAs) direct responsible officials to develop performance metrics to provide data and determine how to overcome challenges to monitoring the transportation systems sector's cybersecurity progress; and
- Administrator of the Environmental Protection Agency direct responsible officials to develop performance metrics to provide data and determine how to overcome challenges to monitoring the water and wastewater systems sector's cybersecurity progress.

Agency Comments and Our Evaluation

We provided a draft of this report to the Departments of Agriculture, Defense, Energy, Health and Human Services, Homeland Security, Transportation, and the Treasury and to EPA. In written comments signed by the Director, Departmental GAO-OIG Liaison Office, DHS concurred with our two recommendations. DHS also provided details about efforts to address cybersecurity in the sectors for which DHS has responsibility as the SSA. DHS also stated that it supports the intent of the recommendation to improve cybersecurity, including efforts to develop performance metrics. Further, in regard to the transportation sector specifically, DHS stated that the Transportation Security Administration and the United States Coast Guard would work in collaboration with the Department of Transportation to ensure that cybersecurity is at the forefront of their voluntary partnership.

In written comments signed by the Department of the Treasury's Acting Assistant Secretary for Financial Institutions, the department stated that monitoring the sector's cybersecurity progress is a critical component of the sector's efforts to reduce cybersecurity risk and discussed efforts with the department's partners to improve the sector's ability to assess progress and develop metrics.

In written comments signed by EPA's Deputy Assistant Administrator, EPA generally agreed with our recommendation and discussed efforts to develop cybersecurity performance metrics for the water and wastewater systems sector.

The Department of Transportation's Director of Program Management and Improvement stated in an e-mail that the department concurred with our findings and our recommendation directed to the Secretary of Transportation and stated that it would continue to work with DHS to improve cyber risk mitigation activities and strengthen the transportation sector's cybersecurity posture.

If effectively implemented, the actions identified by these departments should help address the need to better measure cybersecurity progress in the sectors.

The Departments of Agriculture and Health and Human Services did not comment on the recommendations made to them.

In addition, officials from the Departments of Agriculture, Defense, Energy, Health and Human Services, Homeland Security, and the Treasury and EPA also provided technical comments via e-mail that have been addressed in this report as appropriate. The Department of Transportation did not have technical comments for the report.

Gregory C. Wilshusen
Director, Information Security Issues

Appendix I: Objectives, Scope, and Methodology

Our objectives were to determine the extent to which sector-specific agencies (SSA) have (1) identified the significance of cyber risks to their respective sectors' networks and industrial control systems, (2) taken actions to mitigate cyber risks within their respective sectors, (3) collaborated across sectors to improve cybersecurity, and (4) established performance metrics to monitor improvements in their respective sectors.

To conduct our evaluation, we analyzed relevant critical infrastructure protection policies and guidance for improving the cybersecurity posture of the nation's critical infrastructure. Based on these analyses, we identified nine federal agencies designated as the sector-specific agencies for the critical infrastructure sectors. For this review, we focused on eight of the nine sector-specific agencies responsible for 15 of the 16 critical infrastructure sectors. We included the 15 sectors that involve private sector stakeholders in their efforts to implement activities to address sector security and resiliency goals. We excluded the General Services Administration, the sector-specific agency for the government facilities sector, as the sector is uniquely governmental with facilities either owned or leased by government entities. See Table 8 for the sectors and sector-specific agencies included in our review.

To determine how sector-specific agencies prioritized cyber risks, we analyzed their efforts to identify and document cyber risks. We reviewed the risk assessment methodologies employed as documented in the 2010 sector-specific plans and other supplementary documentation such as formal risk assessments, strategy documents, and annual reports. We also interviewed officials responsible for carrying out the sector-specific agency roles and responsibilities to further understand their determination of the significance of cyber-related risks to their respective sectors.

To identify SSAs' activities to mitigate cyber risks, we compared sector-specific planning documents and actions to fulfill roles and responsibilities as identified in federal policy and the 2013 National Infrastructure Protection Plan (NIPP) Call to Action steps related to cyber risks. The NIPP steps are suggested practices to guide sector-specific agencies' actions. The NIPP presented a total of 12 steps; however, we excluded 2 steps that we determined did not have a cybersecurity-related nexus.[43] We analyzed the latest sector-specific plans, which were released in 2010, and other sector-specific planning documents including risk assessments and strategies for each of the sectors. We also interviewed officials from the SSAs and obtained related documentation to identify cyber risk mitigation activities. Additionally, we interviewed private sector stakeholders representing the sector coordinating councils to corroborate the sector-specific agencies cyber risk mitigation activities. We used all of this information to determine the extent to which each of the sector-specific agencies conducted activities for the 9 of the NIPP Call to Action steps.[44]

To determine the extent of the sector-specific agencies' collaborative efforts to enhance their sectors' cybersecurity environment, we reviewed documentation related to the collaboration mechanisms utilized by the sector-specific agencies. We also identified the collaborative groups, councils, and working groups that were utilized most frequently by SSAs to share cybersecurity-related information across the sectors. We analyzed documentation of cross-sector collaboration from the sector, government, and cross-sector coordinating councils. Additionally, we interviewed SSA officials and private sector stakeholders representing the sector coordinating councils.

Table 8. Critical Infrastructure Sectors in the Scope of this Review and their Associated Sector-Specific Agency

Sector	Sector-specific agency
1. Chemical	Department of Homeland Security
2. Commercial facilities	Department of Homeland Security
3. Communications	Department of Homeland Security
4. Critical manufacturing	Department of Homeland Security
5. Dams	Department of Homeland Security
6. Defense industrial base	Department of Defense
7. Emergency services	Department of Homeland Security
8. Energy	Department of Energy
9. Financial services	Department of the Treasury
10. Food and Agriculture	Departments of Agriculture and Health and Human Services
11. Health care and public health	Department of Health and Human Services
12. Information technology	Department of Homeland Security
13. Nuclear reactors, materials, and waste	Department of Homeland Security
14. Transportation systems	Transportation Security Administration/US Coast Guard (DHS) and Department of Transportation
15. Water and wastewater systems	Environmental Protection Agency

Source: Presidential Policy Directive 21. | GAO-16-79

To identify performance measures used by SSAs to monitor cybersecurity in their respective sectors, we analyzed the sector-specific plans and cybersecurity-related performance reporting documents and interviewed SSA officials. We reviewed performance evaluation guidance related to national security and resiliency goals provided to the SSAs for past and future planning efforts. Additionally, we reviewed past sector annual reports, which tracked actions of the sector against goals established in the 2010 sector-specific plans, as well as strategic documents or roadmaps used to track sector performance. We reviewed reports of cyber incidents and data breaches provided as examples of indicators for SSAs to monitor sector cybersecurity. We also interviewed private sector partners to identify sources of cybersecurity-related data being reported to the sector-specific agencies.

We conducted this performance audit from June 2014 to November 2015 in accordance with generally accepted government auditing standards. Those standards require that we plan and perform the audit to obtain sufficient, appropriate evidence to provide a reasonable basis for our findings and conclusions based on our audit objectives. We believe the evidence obtained provides a reasonable basis for our findings and conclusions based on our audit objectives.

APPENDIX II: SECTOR-SPECIFIC AGENCIES' CYBER RISK MITIGATION ACTIVITIES BY SECTOR

This appendix provides further details on cyber risk mitigation activities sector-specific agencies (SSA) developed for the 15 sectors in our review based on analysis of documentation and statements from SSA officials. Tables 9 through 23 below show, for each sector, SSA actions that aligned with the 2013 National Infrastructure Protection Plan (NIPP) Call to Action Steps.

Table 9. Chemical Sector Cyber Risk Mitigation Activities

Sector-specific agency: Department of Homeland Security (DHS)	
Call to Action steps	**Activities for the sector**
Build Upon Partnerships	
Determine Collective Actions through Joint Planning Efforts	• Developed the 2010 chemical sector-specific plan through the partnership and working relationships with the sector and government coordinating councils. It detailed the sector's first goal to evaluate the security posture of the sector's high- risk

Call to Action steps	Activities for the sector
	assets, to include cyber elements. • Developed, in collaboration with the sector coordinating council, the Playbook for an Effective All-Hazards Chemical Sector Response, which provides a standard operating procedure to assist the sector in preparing for, responding to, and recovering from all-hazards emergencies. • Released a roadmap in 2009 as voluntary guidance to improve cybersecurity in the sector.[a] • Partnered in 2012 with the Chemical sector coordinating council to complete and distribute Making the Business Case, a document which encourages companies to improve overall security.
Empower Local and Regional Partnerships to Build Capacity	• Worked, in partnership with the American Chemistry Council's Chemical Information Technology Center's Cyber Security Program,[b] to exchange information on cybersecurity concerns and participate in government-sponsored partnership programs. • Supported efforts by chemical facility owners and operators to assess the risks, including those to systems and networks, associated with their facilities. For example, if a facility is at risk for significant potential consequences, it is to complete the Chemical Security Assessment Tool Security Vulnerability Assessment to assess the vulnerability and consequences for cyber assets.
Leverage Incentives to Advance Security and Resilience	• None identified.
Innovate in Managing Risk	
Enable Risk-Informed Decision Making through Enhanced Situational Awareness	• Participated in the Cross-Sector Cybersecurity Working Group and Industrial Control Systems Joint Working Group to address cybersecurity challenges through exchange of cross-sector perspectives and to discuss and address cybersecurity issues that impact industrial control systems. • Participated on the Federal Senior Leadership Council. • Sponsored various information-sharing mechanisms including monthly suspicious/threat activity teleconferences, the Homeland Security Information Network-Critical Sectors, and the DHS Office of Cybersecurity and Communications Spotlight publication, according to DHS officials. • Used the Industrial Control Systems Cyber Emergency Response Team to disseminate information and alerts to provide situational awareness on cyber incidents.
Analyze Infrastructure Dependencies, Interdependencies, and Associated Cascading Effects	• Collaborated through the Cross-Sector Cybersecurity Working Group and with other sector-specific agencies through the Federal Senior Leadership Council to address cybersecurity challenges through the exchange of cross-sector perspectives on interdependencies, among other things.
Identify, Assess, and Respond to Unanticipated Infrastructure Cascading Effects During and Following Incidents	• Directed in the Chemical Sector Security Awareness Guide how sector owners and operators should report cyber incidents and vulnerabilities to the United States Computer Emergency Readiness Team, to respond to and analyze cyber incidents.

Table 9. (Continued)

Call to Action steps	Activities for the sector
	• Promoted sector business continuity planning training, business continuity and disaster recovery planning tools, and exercises to inform a business continuity plan.
Strengthen Coordinated Development and Delivery of Technical Assistance, Training, and Education	• Compiled, in partnership with industry, training and reference information to assist owners in addressing industrial control systems security, including the Roadmap to Secure Control Systems in the Chemical Sector; Industrial Control Systems IncidentResponse and Reporting: Suggested Cybersecurity Procurement Language for Control Systems; the Chemical Sector Industrial Control Systems Security Training Resource Guide; Industrial Control Systems Standards and Guidelines; and the Industrial Control Systems Cyber Emergency Response Team Cybersecurity Evaluation Tool. • Promoted a cybersecurity tabletop exercise to educate owners. • Promoted sector use of the web-based Chemical Security Awareness Training Program to increase security awareness at chemical facilities nationwide.
Improve Critical Infrastructure Security and Resilience by Advancing Research and Development Solutions	• Worked to identify research and development requirements, initiatives, and gaps for the chemical sector. • Participated with the Institute for Information Infrastructure Protection on cybersecurity research topics such as the survivability and recovery of process controls; business rationale for cybersecurity; safeguarding digital identity; human behavior, insider threat, and awareness; and security incentives through risk pricing.
Focus on Outcomes	
Learn and Adapt During and After Exercises and Incidents	• Participated in national-level cybersecurity exercises, such as Cyber Storm, which provided the opportunity for sector participants to exercise strategic decision making, interagency coordination of incident responses, and information-sharing processes for collecting and disseminating cyber incident situational awareness across sectors.

Source: GAO analysis of agency information. | GAO-16-79

[a] DHS, Roadmap to Secure Control Systems in the Chemical Sector (September 2009).

[b] The American Chemistry Council's Chemical Information Technology Center's Cyber Security Program provides an information-sharing forum for American Chemistry Council.

Table 10. Commercial Facilities Sector Cyber Risk Mitigation Activities

Sector-specific agency: Department of Homeland Security (DHS)	
Call to Action steps	**Activities for the sector**
Build Upon Partnerships	
Determine Collective Actions through Joint Planning Efforts	• Established the Commercial Facilitates Information Sharing and Analysis Center.

Call to Action steps	Activities for the sector
	• Started the Commercial Facilities Cyber Working Group to enhance cyber engagement throughout the sector and promote NIST's Framework for Improving Critical Infrastructure Cybersecurity. • Developed the 2010 Commercial Facilities Sector-Specific Plan in coordination with public and private sector partners.
Empower Local and Regional Partnerships to Build Capacity	• Coordinated with the Department of State and other DHS components, and has ongoing plans to conduct international outreach activities to promote the adoption of best practices designed to improve the protection of the sector. • Conducted an annual assessment of the key risks to the sector from a national perspective; the Strategic Homeland Infrastructure Risk Analysis report identifies those hazards that pose the greatest risk to the sector as a whole or which would produce a national impact.
Leverage Incentives to Advance Security and Resilience	• None identified.
Innovate in Managing Risk	
Enable Risk-Informed Decision Making through Enhanced Situational Awareness	• Worked with DHS Office of Cyber Security and Communications to support a number of information-sharing mechanisms. These include the United States Computer Emergency Readiness Team, Industrial Control Systems Cyber Emergency Response Team, Homeland Security Information Network—Commercial Facilities, Homeland Security Information Network Connect Page, e-mail lists, government coordinating council, sector coordinating council, and Commercial Facilities Cyber Working Group. • Established a cybersecurity working group with the support of the DHS Office of Cybersecurity and Communications to share cybersecurity information. • Participated in the Office of Infrastructure Protection Cross-Sector Cyber Security working group.
Analyze Infrastructure Dependencies, Interdependencies, and Associated Cascading Effects	• Worked with its sector partners and Infrastructure Information Collection Division to identify those data infrastructure elements necessary for understanding the sector's infrastructure dependencies and interdependencies. • Used the Infrastructure Data Warehouse and has taken a comprehensive, integrated view of the sector's infrastructure, including all of its characteristics and the dependencies necessary for it to function.
Identify, Assess, and Respond to Unanticipated Infrastructure Cascading Effects During and Following Incidents	• Identified the sector's critical cybersecurity functions and services as part of the Cyber-Dependent Infrastructure Identification effort called for by Executive Order 13636.
Strengthen Coordinated Development and Delivery of Technical Assistance, Training, and Education	• Developed a risk self-assessment tool in conjunction with the International Association of Assembly Managers and Infrastructure Information Collection Division that contains cyber-risk assessment sections to makes sector partners aware of the importance of their cyber systems and suggest protective programs that can be implemented to respond to cyber threats.

Table 10. (Continued)

Call to Action steps	Activities for the sector
	• Worked with sector partners to develop several risk assessment tools and assessment reports that address the risks that are of concern to the sector. • Coordinated with other organizational elements within the Office of Infrastructure Protection to develop training and education products across the critical infrastructuresectors and to participate in conferences, workshops, and other outreach and educational events. • Developed materials to guide the sector in implementing cybersecurity protective measures, such as the Protective Measures Guide and Training Guide (Cyberterrorism Defense Initiative and ACT Online).
Improve Critical Infrastructure Security and Resilience by Advancing Research and Development Solutions	• Increased outreach at the corporate level to identify sector cybersecurity gaps, guide sector cybersecurity priorities, and identify resources to fill the identified gaps. The sector-specific agency is also re-introducing an effort to expand an existing Cybersecurity Working Group.
Focus on Outcomes	
Learn and Adapt During and After Exercises and Incidents	• Worked with the sector to develop and participate in sector-specific, as well as national level, cross-sector exercises, which include Top Officials Exercises series, the National Level Exercise, and Cyber Storm II. These initiatives provide critically important measures for the state of preparedness, information sharing, and incident management procedures and protocols.

Source: GAO analysis of agency information. | GAO-16-79

Table 11. Communications Sector Cyber Risk Mitigation Activities

Sector-specific agency: Department of Homeland Security (DHS)	
Call to Action steps	**Activities for the sector**
Build Upon Partnerships	
Determine Collective Actions through Joint Planning Efforts	• Outlined, in the 2010 sector-specific plan, cyber infrastructure protection activities to mitigate risks to critical national communications infrastructure assets and services. • Participated, with the sector partners, in exercises to test and implement network- level protective strategies, including tabletop exercise executed in support of the National Cyber Incident Response Plan.
Empower Local and Regional Partnerships to Build Capacity	• Facilitated forums, through DHS's Critical Infrastructure Cyber Community Voluntary Program, for local and regional partners to discuss evolving cyber risk management issues. • Assessed, in collaboration with sector partners and the sector coordinating council, risk using the National Sector Risk Assessment for Communications.[a] • Participated with sector partners in cyber exercises, including Cyber Storm.

Call to Action steps	Activities for the sector
Leverage Incentives to Advance Security and Resilience	• None identified.
Innovate in Managing Risk	
Enable Risk-Informed Decision Making through Enhanced Situational Awareness	• Collaborated across sectors to improve cybersecurity postures, including through the Communications Sector Outreach and Awareness Webinar Series; Federal Communications Commission sponsored Communications Security, Reliability andInteroperability Council's Best Practices Working Group activities; and Federal Senior Leadership Council meetings with the other sector-specific agencies for the other 15 critical infrastructure sectors. • Provided information to the sector through regularly scheduled meetings, bulletins, Structured Threat Information Expression and Trusted Automated Exchange of Indicator Information, the National Cybersecurity and Communications Integration Center, the National Infrastructure Coordinating Center, and the National Coordinating Center for Telecommunications and Communications-Information Sharing and Analysis Center.
Analyze Infrastructure Dependencies, Interdependencies, and Associated Cascading Effects	• Facilitated, in collaboration with sector partners, communications dependency analyses for other critical infrastructure sectors by performing assessments that evaluated facilities' communications resilience.
Identify, Assess, and Respond to Unanticipated Infrastructure Cascading Effects During and Following Incidents	• Worked to enhance response and recovery efforts and analyze cyber incident consequences with the Information Technology sector and the National Cybersecurity and Communications Integration Center. • Worked with sector coordination groups on procedures for sector and cross-sector incident management and the sharing of situational awareness information during incidents.
Strengthen Coordinated Development and Delivery of Technical Assistance, Training, and Education	• Shared training information with the sector and government coordinating council via e-mail. • Contributed to the development of the National Institute of Standards and Technology (NIST) Cybersecurity Framework through NIST's requests for information process. • Held a webinar presenting information on the Critical Infrastructure Cyber Community Voluntary Program in March 2015. • Leveraged resources to enhance the sector's overall cyber posture and critical infrastructure protection efforts.
Improve Critical Infrastructure Security and Resilience by Advancing Research and Development Solutions	• Worked with sector partners toprioritize research and development efforts.
Focus on Outcomes	
Learn and Adapt During and After Exercises and Incidents	• Conducted internal and external exercises for maintaining expert knowledge of and proficiency in the management, integration, and use of national security and emergency preparedness communications resources.

Source: GAO analysis of agency information. | GAO-16-79

[a] The National Sector Risk Assessment informs the sector protection and resiliency activities and aims to inform public and private decision-makers and stakeholders of the evolving risks to the

communications sector, improve the security and resiliency of the Nation's communications systems, and assist decision-makers and stakeholders reduce risk across the communications sector.

Table 12. Critical Manufacturing Sector Cyber Risk Mitigation Activities

Sector-specific agency: Department of Homeland Security (DHS)	
Call to Action steps	**Activities for the sector**
Build Upon Partnerships	
Determine Collective Actions through Joint Planning Efforts	• Worked with the Office of Cyber Security and Communications to provide guidance and assistance regarding cybersecurity incidents. • Updated the 2010 sector-specific plan and determined that cybersecurity was not a priority for the sector but noted that future iterations would reconsider cybersecurity's importance to the sector.
Empower Local and Regional Partnerships to Build Capacity Nationally	• Participated in the Strategic Homeland Infrastructure Risk Analysis conducted by • Homeland Infrastructure Threat and Risk Analysis Center. • Led development of a regional sector coordinating council outreach model to encourage partnerships with geographically diverse, small and medium-sized sector partners that are not a part of the current sector coordinating council membership. • Increased federal partnership by reaching out to representatives from federal agencies and the State, Local, Tribal, and Territorial government coordinating council to expand the Critical Manufacturing government coordinating council.
Leverage Incentives to Advance Security and Resilience	• None identified.
Innovate in Managing Risk	
Enable Risk-Informed Decision Making through Enhanced Situational Awareness	• Participated in the Critical Manufacturing sector coordinating council's cybersecurity working group that meets regularly to discuss current cybersecurity issues.

Call to Action steps	Activities for the sector
Analyze Infrastructure Dependencies, Interdependencies, and Associated Cascading Effects	• Identified dependencies, interdependencies, and overlaps in the 2010 sector- specific planning process to include reliance on the transportation systems sector to transport materials and the energy sector to maintain power to facilities. The plan also notes the interdependency with the emergency services sector that responds to incidents in the critical manufacturing sector and also is supplied with equipment created in that sector.
Identify, Assess, and Respond to Unanticipated Infrastructure Cascading Effects During and Following Incidents	• Participated in the Cyber Exercise Program to help improve the nation's cybersecurity preparedness and incident response capabilities by sponsoring and using findings from exercises and workshops.
Strengthen Coordinated Development and Delivery of Technical Assistance, Training, and Education	• Leveraged existing training produced by DHS's Office of Infrastructure Protection provided as web-based training through the Homeland Security Information Network such as cybersecurity training for sector partners' employees.
Improve Critical Infrastructure Security and Resilience by Advancing Research and Development Solutions	• None identified.
Focus on Outcomes	
Learn and Adapt During and After Exercises and Incidents	• Participated in Cyber Storm, federally- sponsored exercises focused on cybersecurity that, among other things, build upon lessons learned to develop more sophisticated incident response scenarios for future exercises. • Used the DHS's Cyber Exercise Program to assess risk of systems by sponsoring and using findings from national, regional, interagency, and international exercises and workshops.

Source: GAO analysis of agency information. | GAO-16-79

Table 13. Dams Sector Cyber Risk Mitigation Activities

Sector-specific agency: Department of Homeland Security (DHS)	
Call to Action steps	**Activities for the sector**
Build Upon Partnerships	
Determine Collective Actions through Joint Planning Efforts	• Developed the 2010 Dams Sector-Specific Plan through the partnerships and working relationships with the private sector and all levels of government.
Empower Local and Regional Partnerships to Build Capacity	• Participated in sector and government coordinating councils encompassing the private sector, local and state governments, government and privately-owned utility companies, and industry associations.
Leverage Incentives to Advance Security and Resilience	• None identified.
Innovate in Managing Risk	
Enable Risk-Informed Decision Making through Enhanced Situational Awareness	• Facilitated and promoted information sharing within and across the sectors through the DHS's Sector Outreach and Programs Division. • Worked with the cybersecurity working group to discuss cyber-related activities applicable to the sector. Also, shared cyber-related information through online portals and e-mail. • Supported quarterly threat briefings at the unclassified and classified level by providing context and mitigation strategies. • Disseminated DHS Industrial Control System Cyber Emergency Response Team and United States Computer Emergency Readiness Team alerts and advisories to sector partners through e-mail and web portals hosted by the Homeland Security Information Network.
Analyze Infrastructure Dependencies, Interdependencies, and Associated Cascading Effects	• Collaborated through the Cross-Sector Cybersecurity Working Group and Industrial Control System Joint working Group to provide further coordination on cyber- specific issues and cross-sector perspectives and knowledge regarding various cybersecurity concerns.

Call to Action steps	Activities for the sector
Identify, Assess, and Respond to Unanticipated Infrastructure Cascading Effects During and Following Incidents	• Identified critical functions and services as part of the 2013 Cyber-Dependent Infrastructure Identification effort, called for by Executive Order 13636.
Strengthen Coordinated Development and Delivery of Technical Assistance, Training, and Education	• Developed the Roadmap to Secure Control Systems and has ongoing efforts within the Cybersecurity Working Group to update the roadmap to reflect current risks. • Worked on a dams-specific Cybersecurity Framework Implementation Guide to make the National Institute of Standards and Technology Framework for Improving Critical Infrastructure Cybersecurity more relatable to sector stakeholders.
Improve Critical Infrastructure Security and Resilience by Advancing Research and Development Solutions	• Facilitated a research and development workgroup composed of Government Coordinating Council and sector coordinating council members to characterize sector research and technology needs, maintain technology and research related to those needs, and delineate the gaps between what is needed and what is available or known in order to coordinate research and development activities.
Focus on Outcomes	
Learn and Adapt During and After Exercises and Incidents	• Applied lessons learned from other sector-specific agencies to improve cybersecurity-related efforts. For example, the dams sector is currently developing a sector-specific Cybersecurity Capability Maturity Model, updating the 2010 Sector Roadmap to Secure Control Systems, and developing an integrated cyber and physical risk assessment.

Source: GAO analysis of agency information. | GAO-16-79

Table 14. Defense Industrial Base Sector Cyber Risk Mitigation Activities

Sector-specific agency: Department of Defense (DOD)	
Call to Action steps	**Activities for the sector**
Build Upon Partnerships	
Determine Collective Actions through Joint Planning Efforts	• Reported that the sector coordinating council and asset owners are called upon to support risk management activities such as cybersecurity, assurance, and protection with associated implementation actions. • Developed the 2010 Defense Industrial Base sector-specific plan through the partnership and working relationships with the sector and government coordinating councils. It described the sector-specific agency's program elements for cybersecurity, assurance, and protection.
Empower Local and Regional Partnerships to Build Capacity Nationally	• Worked with the Department of Homeland Security (DHS) Protective Security Advisors, who proactively engage with federal, state, local, tribal, and territorial government mission partners and members of the private sector stakeholder community to protect critical infrastructure, to ensure that the owners and operators are coordinating with state and local emergency response entities and other critical infrastructure community members. • Created the Defense Industrial Base Cyber Security/Information Assurance program to mature the public-private cybersecurity partnership within the sector. The program is to enhance and supplement sector participants' capabilities to safeguard DOD information that resides on or transits unclassified networks or information systems within the sector.
Leverage Incentives to Advance Security and Resilience	• None identified.
Innovate in Managing Risk	
Enable Risk-Informed Decision Making through Enhanced Situational Awareness	• Joined the Cross Sector Cybersecurity Working Group. • Provided cyber awareness training modules, cyber threat indicators, cyber bulletins, and

Call to Action steps	Activities for the sector
	mitigation strategies with cleared defense contractors, in some cases, daily or weekly.
Analyze Infrastructure Dependencies, Interdependencies, and Associated Cascading Effects	• Partnered with different federal agencies to oversee cross-sector working groupsand is heavily involved with DHS and its cybersecurity programs. • Partnered with DHS Protective Security Advisors to inform sector owners and operators of local networks and resources to identify their dependencies and associated vulnerabilities.
Identify, Assess, and Respond to Unanticipated Infrastructure Cascading Effects During and Following Incidents	• Developed the Risk Management Framework for DoD Information Technology tool, which provides a decision structure to review cybersecurity posture.
Strengthen Coordinated Development and Delivery of Technical Assistance, Training, and Education	• Worked with the National Institute of Standards and Technology, interagency partners, industry, and the general public in the development of the National Institute of Standards and Technology's (NIST) Framework for Improving Critical Infrastructure Cybersecurity. • Took steps to promote use of NIST's Framework for Improving Critical Infrastructure Cybersecurity. For example, DOD is participating in the interagency effort to explore various incentives that might be offered to industry to encourage use of the framework, as well as actions by the acquisition community to improve cybersecurity in DOD's contracts and other agreements with external vendors.
Improve Critical Infrastructure Security and Resilience by Advancing Research and Development Solutions	• Supported efforts throughout the sector to identify new technology and softwaresolutions for cybersecurity needs.
Focus on Outcomes	
Learn and Adapt During and After Exercises and Incidents	• Participated in DOD-centric exercises as well as national-level exercises. • Shared information and training based on results of internal exercises with contractors and the public.

Source: GAO analysis of agency information. | GAO-16-79

Table 15. Emergency Services Sector Cyber Risk Mitigation Activities

Sector-specific agency: Department of Homeland Security (DHS)	
Call to Action steps	**Activities for the sector**
Build Upon Partnerships	
Determine Collective Actions through Joint Planning Efforts	• Developed the 2010 sector-specific plan to include the importance of factoring cybersecurity components into all critical infrastructure protection-related activities. • Prepared the 2010 Emergency Services Sector Critical Infrastructure and Key Resources Protection Annual Report, which described activities conducted fromMay 1, 2009, to April 30, 2010. • Developed a roadmap in 2013 that identified potential actions to mitigate the risks identified in the emergency services sector cyber risk assessment, according to DHS officials. • Reviewed and contributed to the National Cyber Incident Response Plan.
Empower Local and Regional Partnerships to Build Capacity Nationally	• Collaborated with sector partners including the National Sheriffs'Association, the International Association of Fire Chiefs, the U.S. Department of Transportation's Pipeline and Hazardous Materials Safety Administration, and DHS's Federal Emergency Management Agency. • Encouraged sector-wide participation in DHS's Critical Infrastructure Cyber Community Voluntary Program, according to DHS officials.
Leverage Incentives to Advance Security and Resilience	• None identified.
Innovate in Managing Risk	
Enable Risk-Informed Decision Making through Enhanced Situational Awareness	• Nominated and processed security clearances at the top-secret and secret levels. • Leveraged the Cross-Sector Cyber Security Working Group to promote cybersecurity information sharing, according to DHS officials. • Facilitated information-sharing mechanisms to disseminate cyber threat and vulnerability information to sector partners, including the Homeland Security Information Network Emergency Services, First Responder Community of Practice for Emergency Services Sector, e-mail distribution lists, and meetings of the government and sector coordinating councils.

Call to Action steps	Activities for the sector
	• Promoted, through DHS's Science and Technology Directorate, interoperability between various information sharing platforms to ensure that sector stakeholders are informed and have access to information-sharing solutions that meet their needs during both incidents and steady-state operations.
Analyze Infrastructure Dependencies, Interdependencies, and Associated Cascading Effects	• Participated in monthly meetings to share cross-sector information with agencies that have dependencies and interdependencies with the sector, including the Cross-Sector Information Sharing and Analysis Center meetings and Cross Sector Cybersecurity Working Group's monthly meetings.
Identify, Assess, and Respond to Unanticipated Infrastructure Cascading Effects During and Following Incidents	• Used information-gathering mechanisms from the sector to receive and distribute cybersecurity incident information, including the Homeland Security Information Network-Emergency Services page, the Multi-State-Information Sharing and Analysis Center e-mail lists, and the government and sector coordinating councils, according to DHS officials.
Strengthen Coordinated Development and Delivery of Technical Assistance, Training, and Education	• Participated in various conferences to brief practitioners and association executive staff on protection initiatives to include the National Emergency Numbers Association, National Sheriffs' Association, Interagency Board Executive Council, National Forum on Information Sharing, Fusion Center, American Public Works Association, and the Urban Area Security Initiative. • Worked to complete a draft Emergency Services-specific NIST Cybersecurity Framework Implementation Guide to make the NIST framework more relatable to sector stakeholders, according to DHS officials.
Improve Critical Infrastructure Security and Resilience by Advancing Research and Development Solutions	• Supported the sector's First Responder Coordinating Council, a vehicle for the coordination of investment, programs, technology, research, development, and delivery of technological tools to first responders at the federal, state, local, tribal and territorial levels.
Focus on Outcomes	
Learn and Adapt During and After Exercises and Incidents	• Participated in DHS's Cyber Exercise Program and Cyber Storm Exercises, to evaluate incident response and coordination interdependencies and capabilitiesin response to a large-scale cyber incident. • Supported the Emergency Services Sector Exercise Working Group, which provides a national perspective of lessons learned and value-added results of the exercises.

Source: GAO analysis of agency information. | GAO-16-79

Table 16. Energy Sector Cyber Risk Mitigation Activities

Sector-specific agency: Department of Energy (DOE)	
Call to Action steps	**Activities for the sector**
Build Upon Partnerships	
Determine Collective Actions through Joint Planning Efforts	• Updated the sector-specific plan in 2010 to include the importance of factoring cybersecurity components into all critical infrastructure protection-related activities. • Developed sector-specific cybersecurity framework implementation guidance to assist energy sector organizations in demonstrating and communicating their cybersecurity profile. • Worked with Smart Grid Investment Grant program recipients to encourage development and implementation of cybersecurity plans for strengthening security and resilience.[a]
Empower Local and Regional Partnerships to Build Capacity Nationally	• Encouraged industry participation in both national and regional preparedness projects including cyber exercises and industry work groups. • Led a cyber incident management capability exercise series that focused on regional coordination in the event of cyber incidents. • Coordinated an exercise with a cyber-attack targeting information technology and energy delivery systems in October 2014. According to officials, this exercise had more than 120 executives, managers, and operational staff from industry and government agencies.
Leverage Incentives to Advance Security and Resilience	• Provided incentives to advance security and resilience by supporting cost-shared industry-led research and development of cybersecurity innovation for energy delivery systems technologies and techniques
Innovate in Managing Risk	
Enable Risk-Informed Decision Making through Enhanced Situational Awareness	• Developed and implemented the Cybersecurity Risk Information Sharing Program as a pilot program to enable real-time information sharing. • Implemented the Cyber Fed model program that enables machine-to-machine sharing of cyber threat information amongst the energy subsectors.

Call to Action steps	Activities for the sector
	• Hosted classified and non-classified threat briefings and workshops for industry stakeholders, and looked at further enhancing energy sector information sharing capabilities in alignment with the Executive Order 13691, Promoting Private sector Cybersecurity Information Sharing.
Analyze Infrastructure Dependencies, Interdependencies, and Associated Cascading Effects	• Participated in the Networking Information Technology Research and Development Program, which included research and development coordination topics such as cross-sector cybersecurity interdependencies. • Participated in the development of the Critical Infrastructure Security and ResilienceNational Research and Development Plan,[b] which allowed the sharing of information and increased awareness of interdependencies among critical infrastructure stakeholders.
Identify, Assess, and Respond to Unanticipated Infrastructure Cascading Effects During and Following Incidents	• Updated the 2010 sector-specific plan to include the importance of factoring cybersecurity components into all critical infrastructure protection-related activities. • Designed the Cybersecurity for Energy Delivery Systems program to assist the energy sector asset owners by developing cybersecurity solutions to share information and strengthen awareness of interdependencies among critical infrastructures.
Strengthen Coordinated Development and Delivery of Technical Assistance, Training, and Education	• Worked with industry to develop sector-specific technical assistance, training, and education. In particular, through an industry workshop in 2013, identified cybersecurity workforce competencies. • Partnered with DHS's Science and Technology Directorate to support the Trustworthy Cyber Infrastructure for the Power Grid Collaboration Project,[c] which developed and provided training modules for cybersecurity of energy delivery systems. • Developed sector-specific implementation guidance to promote adoption of NIST's Framework for Improving Critical Infrastructure Cybersecurity throughout the sector.

Table 16. (Continued)

Call to Action steps	Activities for the sector
	• Developed the Roadmap to Achieve Energy Delivery Systems Cybersecurity to support energy delivery systems that are designed, installed, operated and maintained to survive a cyber-incident while sustaining critical functions. • Hosted two workshops between 2011 and 2013 to share information and lessons learned in developing and implementing cybersecurity plans and sustaining cybersecurity processes.
Improve Critical Infrastructure Security and Resilience by Advancing Research and Development Solutions	• Participated in the development of the National Critical Infrastructure Security and Resilience Research and Development Plan, which presents strategic guidance across all critical infrastructure sectors.
	• Provided incentives to advance security and resilience by supporting cost-shared industry-led research and development of cybersecurity innovation for energy delivery systems technologies and techniques.
Focus on Outcomes	
Learn and Adapt During and After Exercises and Incidents	• Participated in North American Electric Reliability Corporation's Grid Security Exercise and the Dams Sector Information Sharing Drill. • Led the Cyber Incident Management Capabilities Exercise in October 2014, which incorporated lessons learned and potential challenges from past exercises into theexercise scenario.

Source: GAO analysis of agency information. | GAO-16-79

[a] The American Recovery and Reinvestment Act of 2009 provided DOE with $4.5 billion to modernize the electric power grid. The Smart Grid Investment Grant program is authorized by the Energy Independence and Security Act of 2007, Section 1306, as amended by the Recovery Act. The purpose of the grant program is to accelerate the modernization of the nation's electric transmission and distribution systems and promote investments in smart grid technologies, tools, and techniques that increase flexibility, functionality, interoperability, cybersecurity, situational awareness, and operational efficiency.

[b] National Infrastructure Advisory Council, Critical Infrastructure Security and Resilience National Research and Development Plan (November 14, 2014).

[c] The Trustworthy Cyber Infrastructure for the Power Grid Collaboration Project is a DOE-funded collaborative initiative with academic institutions to research new technologies that, among other things, could detect and respond to cyber attacks.

Table 17. Financial Services Sector Cyber Risk Mitigation Activities

Sector-specific agency: Department of the Treasury	
Call to Action steps	**Activities for the sector**
Build Upon Partnerships	
Determine Collective Actions through Joint Planning Efforts	• Updated the 2010 sector-specific plan to include the importance of factoring cybersecurity components into all critical infrastructure protection-related activities. • Collaborated with sector partners' to provide input to the draft National Cyber Incident Response Plan.[a] • Used the Financial Services Sector All-Hazards Crisis Response Playbook to coordinate response efforts within the sector.
Call to Action steps	**Activities for the sector**
Empower Local and Regional Partnerships to Build Capacity	• Engaged with sector partners through the sector coordinating council and Financial and Banking Information Infrastructure Committee (FBIIC)[b] cybersecurity committees to address the sector's cybersecurity needs. • Leveraged the sector regulators' risk assessments to assess sector-wide risks. • Participated in several cyber exercises to demonstrate an integrated applicationof risk management and planning, such as the Quantum Dawn series of exercises in 2011 and 2013.[c]
Leverage Incentives to Advance Security and Resilience	• None identified.
Innovate in Managing Risk	
Enable Risk-Informed Decision Making through Enhanced Situational Awareness	• Worked collaboratively with FBIIC members and other sectors to accomplish Cross-Sector Cyber Security Working Group activities and with the Federal Communications Commission's Communications Security,

Table 17. (Continued)

Call to Action steps	Activities for the sector
	Reliability Interoperability Council due to the sectors' dependence on communications. • Participated in quarterly meetings of the Federal Senior Leadership Council. • Supported the sector coordinating council's efforts to disseminate information, including cybersecurity-related information, through regional coalitions.
Analyze Infrastructure Dependencies, Interdependencies, and Associated Cascading Effects	• Corresponded with industry partners to identify sector dependencies. In particular, due to the sector's dependence on the electric utilities, Treasury worked closely with the Energy SSA and the Federal Communications Commission's Communications Security, Reliability, Interoperability Council.
Identify, Assess, and Respond to Unanticipated Infrastructure Cascading Effects During and Following Incidents	• Worked with law enforcement and industry partners to share actionable, cyber-technical information during response and recovery efforts following incidents. • Assisted the sector in developing continuity plans by creating continuity exercises based on the scenarios in the sector's All-Hazards Playbook according to Treasury officials.
Strengthen Coordinated Development and Delivery of Technical Assistance, Training, and Education	• Conducted briefings with members of the FBIIC and the private sector on the latest intelligence and threat assessments. • Assessed cyber threats with the Department of Homeland Security (DHS). For example, during distributed denial-of-service attacks on the sector in 2012, firms that had not been attacked wanted to understand how the cyber-attack occurred. • Co-sponsored with DHS's Office of Science and Technology, the National Science Foundation, and experts from the sector coordinating council, a workshop that allowed financial services partners to develop a shared view of a resilient cyber infrastructure and next steps for achieving that vision.

Call to Action steps	Activities for the sector
Improve Critical Infrastructure Security and Resilience by Advancing Research and Development Solutions	• Involved in DHS's Apex Project, a research effort that looks at the nation's security and address future challenges, which has been informed of the financial sector's research and development priorities.
Focus on Outcomes	
Learn and Adapt During and After Exercises and Incidents	• Encouraged sector partners to participate in cyber exercises including the Financial Services-Information Sharing and Analysis Center's Cyber Attack (against) Payment Processes exercise; the U.S. National Guard's Cyber Guard exercise; DHS's Cyber Storm, and government-wide continuity exercises according to Treasury officials. • Developed after action reports following exercises that identified key lessons learned and worked on a plan that specified how to implement the lessons learned according to Treasury officials.

Source: GAO analysis of agency information. | GAO-16-79

[a] DHS, National Cyber Incident Response Plan Interim Version (September 2010).

[b] The FBIIC, chaired by Treasury, is chartered under the President's Working Group on Financial Markets, and is charged with improving coordination and communication among financial regulators, enhancing the resiliency of the financial sector, and promoting the public/private partnership.

[c] Quantum Dawn was a cybersecurity exercise to test incident response, resolution and coordination processes for the financial services sector and the individual member firms to a street-wide cyber attack.

Table 18. Food and Agriculture Sector Cyber Risk Mitigation Activities

Sector-specific agencies: U.S. Department of Agriculture (USDA) and Department of Health and Human Services (HHS)	
Call to Action steps	**Activities for the sector**
Build Upon Partnerships	
Determine Collective Actions through Joint Planning Efforts	• Updated the 2010 sector-specific plan and determined that cybersecurity was not a priority for the sector but noted that future iterations would reconsider cybersecurity's importance to the sector.

Table 18. (Continued)

Call to Action steps	Activities for the sector
Empower Local and Regional Partnerships to Build Capacity	• Encouraged sector-wide participation in the Department of Homeland Security's (DHS) Critical Infrastructure Cyber Community Voluntary Program to support cyber resilience and increase awareness and use of the National Institute of Standards and Technology's (NIST) Framework for Improving Critical Infrastructure Cybersecurity.
Leverage Incentives to Advance Security and Resilience	• None identified.
Innovate in Managing Risk	
Enable Risk-Informed Decision Making through Enhanced Situational Awareness	• Supported quarterly cyber threat briefings to sector partners at the unclassified and the classified level to provide context and mitigation strategies. • Participated in several external working groups with cross-sector representation to provide input to the direction of these groups. These groups included the Cross Sector Cybersecurity Working Group.
Analyze Infrastructure Dependencies, Interdependencies, and Associated Cascading Effects	• Collaborated with DHS to conduct three facilitated sessions with sector stakeholders to identify sector risks using DHS's Cybersecurity and Risk Management Approach.
Identify, Assess, and Respond to Unanticipated Infrastructure Cascading Effects During and Following Incidents	• Participated in the process to identify critical functions and services as part of the 2013 Cyber-Dependent Infrastructure Identification effort, called for by Executive Order 13636.
Strengthen Coordinated Development and Delivery of Technical Assistance, Training, and Education	• Participated in meetings regarding a Food and Agriculture-specific NIST cybersecurity framework implementation guide to make the NIST framework more relatable to food and agriculture stakeholders.
Improve Critical Infrastructure Security and Resilience by Advancing Research and Development Solutions	• None Identified.
Focus on Outcomes	
Learn and Adapt During and After Exercises and Incidents	• None Identified.

Source: GAO analysis of agency information. | GAO-16-79

Table 19. Health Care and Public Health Sector Cyber Risk Mitigation Activities

Sector-specific agency: Department of Health and Human Services (HHS)	
Call to Action steps	**Activities for the sector**
Build upon Partnership Efforts	
Determine Collective Actions through Joint Planning Efforts	• Worked with the sector partners on the 2010 sector-specific plan for the sector to include one cybersecurity-related goal. • Developed a Cyber Security Incident Response Plan Concept of Operations in 2013 that addressed roles and responsibilities for cyber incident response within HHS, defined activation levels for cyber incidents, and described response actions to be taken by HHS components. • Provided subject matter expertise for development of the National Cyber Incident Response Plan.
Empower Local and Regional Partnerships to Build Capacity	• Formed a Cyber Security Working Group with the sector partners to begin development of a cybersecurity strategy to address the sector's unique cyber needs. • Created a security risk assessment tool for large and small businesses within the sector to conduct risk assessments on their facilities. • Coordinated, in conjunction with the Health Information Trust Alliance,[a] a series of no cost, industry-wide regional exercises, called Cyber RX.
Leverage Incentives to Advance Security and Resilience	• Identified incentives for participating in the sector's cybersecurity programs, including being granted a security clearance through the private sector clearance program, participating in the government telecommunications and wireless priority programs, having access to classified information, and complying with regulations.
Innovate in Managing Risk	
Enable Risk-Informed Decision Making through Enhanced Situational Awareness	• Worked with the Federal Bureau of Investigation (FBI) to conduct cybersecurity threat briefing for sector partners at FBI field offices. • Participated with sector partners in several Department of Homeland Security (DHS)

Table 19. (Continued)

Call to Action steps	Activities for the sector
	cross-sector groups. For example, HHS officials stated that they attended the Industrial Control Systems Joint Working Group, and presented information during a Health and Public Health focused panel discussions in June 2015. • Monitored health-related critical infrastructure protection information sources and posted relevant content to the Homeland Security Information Network-Healthcare and Public Health portal. • Worked closely with sector partners and DHS's Industrial Control Systems Cyber Emergency Response Team to receive from and distribute to sector members vulnerability awareness information and mitigation strategies.
Analyze Infrastructure Dependencies, Interdependencies, and Associated Cascading Effects	• Attended cross-sector meetings with the financial services, water and wastewater systems; emergency services; and energy sectors to share and receive information related to understanding interdependencies. • Sponsored officials from the financial services and energy sectors to speak on cybersecurity issues during the sector's annual in-person meeting.
Identify, Assess, and Respond to Unanticipated Infrastructure Cascading Effects During and Following Incidents	• Worked closely with DHS's National Cybersecurity and Communications Integration Center, including having staff in the center. • Served on the Cybersecurity Unified Coordination Group for the coordination of cyber incident response in the sector. • Provided contingency training for sector owners and operators following incidents through their website.
Strengthen Coordinated Development and Delivery of Technical Assistance, Training, and Education	• Performed cybersecurity related outreach and educational activities, including presenting at industry conferences, hosting knowledge-sharing sessions with subject matter experts, conducting webinars, and presenting classified briefings. • Provided training and technical assistance resources, such as risk assessment toolsand training videos on a variety of topic areas, to include emergency preparedness, contingency planning, and mobile device security.

Call to Action steps	Activities for the sector
	• Presented on the National Institute of Standards and Technology Framework for Improving Critical Infrastructure Cybersecurity at major national sector meetings, such as the Public Health Preparedness Summit, the Healthcare Information Management System Society Conference, the Public Health Informatics Conference, and the Safeguarding Health Information conference. • Collaborated with educational institutions to review and provide input to critical infrastructure related courses and curriculum. For example, HHS worked with the Federal Emergency Management Agency and other agencies to develop training programs and provide feedback on courses related to the sector and critical infrastructure protection.
Improve Critical Infrastructure Security and Resilience by Advancing Research and Development Solutions	• None identified.
Focus on Outcomes	
Learn and Adapt During and After Exercises and Incidents	• Participated in CyberRx, a set of industry-wide exercises, to simulate cyber-attacks on health care organizations in order to evaluate the industry's response and threat preparedness against attacks and attempts to disrupt U.S. health care industry operations. • Analyzed and used CyberRx findings to identify areas for improvement in Cyber Threat Intelligence and Incident Coordination; with security and incident response programs; and in information sharing between health care organizations, health care cybersecurity-sharing organizations, and government agencies.

Source: GAO analysis of agency information. | GAO-16-79

[a] The Health Information Trust Alliance is an organization that in collaboration with health care, business, technology and information security leaders established the Common Security Framework which can be used by organizations to manage personal health and financial health information.

Table 20. Information Technology Sector Cyber Risk Mitigation Activities

Sector-specific agency: Department of Homeland Security (DHS)	
Call to Action steps	**Activities for the sector**
Build Upon Partnerships	
Determine Collective Actions through Joint Planning Efforts	• Developed, in coordination with the sector and government coordinating councils, the 2010 sector-specific plan, which is concerned with all-hazard events that have cyber and physical consequences. • Assessed the sector's risk, including cyber risk, using the IT Sector Baseline Risk Assessment developed jointly with the sector and government coordinating councils.
Empower Local and Regional Partnerships to Build Capacity Nationally	• Engaged sector partners and other interested sectors through DHS's Critical Infrastructure Cyber Community Voluntary Program by facilitating forums for sector partners to discuss evolving cyber risk management.[a] • Encouraged sector participation in national cyber exercises, such as Cyber Storm.
Leverage Incentives to Advance Security and Resilience	• None identified.
Innovate in Managing Risk	
Enable Risk-Informed Decision Making through Enhanced Situational Awareness	• Participated, along with their sector partners, in cross-sector security policy forums, including the Partnership for Critical Infrastructure Security, Cross-Sector Cybersecurity Working Group, Industrial Control Systems Joint Working Group, and Network Security Information Exchange, to address common cybersecurity challenges and opportunities across the critical infrastructure sectors. • Participated in the quarterly meetings of the Federal Senior Leadership Council. • Disseminated information across the sector via scheduled meetings, bulletins, Structured Threat Information Expression and Trusted Automated Exchange of Indicator Information.[b]

Call to Action steps	Activities for the sector
	• Used operational information sharing mechanisms, such as the United States Computer Emergency Readiness Team and Information Technology-Information Sharing and Analysis Center, to improve incident response and coordinate cybersecurity information sharing.
Analyze Infrastructure Dependencies, Interdependencies, and Associated Cascading Effects	• Identified and analyzed dependencies and interdependencies among the sector's six critical functions and the effects that could occur should those sectors be attacked.[c]
Identify, Assess, and Respond to Unanticipated Infrastructure Cascading Effects During and Following Incidents	• Enhanced response and recovery efforts and analyzed cyber incident consequences by working with the National Cybersecurity and Communications Integration Center. • Coordinated with other DHS components to promote response and recovery by having sector stakeholders located in the National Cybersecurity and Communications Integration Center share information and coordinate response strategies in real time. • Promoted continuity of operations through the Cyber Exercise Program by allowing sector partners to validate their continuity of operations capabilities through participation in exercises.
Strengthen Coordinated Development and Delivery of Technical Assistance, Training, and Education	• Designed programs to promote cybersecurity and resilience across the nation's cyber infrastructure. For example, through the Critical Infrastructure Cyber Community Voluntary Program, DHS organized forums for knowledge sharing and collaboration, and freely accessible technical assistance, tools and resources, among other things. • Responded to the National Institute of Standards and Technology's request for information in support of the development of the Framework for Improving Critical Infrastructure Cybersecurity. Provided information on risk management practices, use of existing frameworks, standards, and best

Table 20. (Continued)

Call to Action steps	Activities for the sector
	practices to manage cybersecurity risk, and industry-specific practices of particular relevance. • Co-sponsored the National Center for Academic Excellence in Information Assurance Education with the National Security Agency and the Federal Cyber Service: Scholarship for Service Program with the National Science Foundation.
Improve Critical Infrastructure Security and Resilience by Advancing Research and Development Solutions	• Prioritized sector's research and development efforts; however, DHS officials stated that, due to the concern for protecting proprietary information in the sector's research and development efforts, they have had only high-level discussions with their private sector partners about the sector's research and development efforts.
Focus on Outcomes	
Learn and Adapt During and After Exercises and Incidents	• Developed, designed, and conducted cyber exercises at the federal, state, regional,and international level. • Leveraged lessons learned from real world cyber incidents through participation in the Cyber Storm exercises.

Source: GAO analysis of agency information. | GAO-16-79

[a] The Critical Infrastructure Cyber Community Voluntary Program was created out of Executive Order13636, Improving Critical Infrastructure Cybersecurity, to help improve the resilience of critical infrastructure cybersecurity systems by supporting and promoting use of the National Institute of Standards and Technology Framework for Improving Critical Infrastructure Cybersecurity.

[b] STIX and TAXII are used to define and develop a standardized language to represent structured cyber threat information and transport the cyber threat information between organizations.

[c] The Information Technology sector's six critical functions are to (1) provide IT products and services; (2) provide incident management capabilities; (3) provide domain name services; (4) provide identify management and associated trust support services; (5) provide Internet-based content, information, and communications services; and (6) provide Internet routing, access, and connection services.

Table 21. Nuclear Reactors, Material, and Waste Sector Cyber Risk Mitigation Activities

Sector-specific agency: Department of Homeland Security (DHS)	
Call to Action steps	**Activities for the sector**
Build Upon Partnerships	
Determine Collective Actions through Joint Planning Efforts	• Worked with the Nuclear Sector Joint Cyber Sub-council[a] in 2011 to develop the Roadmap to Enhance Cyber Systems Security in the Nuclear Sector, a 15-year strategy with activities designed to protect commercial nuclear power from cyber threats and ensure current functional reliability and resilience of the commercial nuclear power subsector.
Empower Local and Regional Partnerships to Build Capacity Nationally	• Supported quarterly meetings of the Nuclear Sector Joint Cyber Sub-council through the Critical Infrastructure Partnership Advisory Council to discuss cyber-related activities applicable to the nuclear sector.
Leverage Incentives to Advance Security and Resilience	• None identified.
Innovate in Managing Risk	
Enable Risk-Informed Decision Making through Enhanced Situational Awareness	• Advanced the appropriate sharing of classified and sensitive information among sector partners including the expansion of the Private Sector Clearance Program, which enabled select sector coordinating council cybersecurity experts to obtain DHS-sponsored top secret clearances. • Collaborated with the Nuclear Sector Joint Cyber Sub-council to add more contextto alerts and advisories provided by entities, such as United States Computer Emergency Readiness Team, so that the sector stakeholders could quickly determine applicability and develop appropriate mitigation strategies. • Facilitated quarterly classified threat briefings to sector partners through DHS's Office of Intelligence and Analysis and active use of the Homeland Security Information Network Critical Sectors portal.

Table 21. (Continued)

Call to Action steps	Activities for the sector
	• Hosted monthly unclassified threat teleconferences and quarterly classified threat briefings with sector partners to discuss relevant threats to the Nuclear Sector and allow private sector representatives to provide context to the information being presented. • Facilitated dissemination of advisories and alerts from the Industrial Control Systems Cyber Emergency Response Team and United States Computer Emergency Readiness Team that identify potential vulnerabilities and risk mitigation strategies.
Analyze Infrastructure Dependencies, Interdependencies, and Associated Cascading Effects	• Identified interdependencies with sectors such as transportation systems and energy through the sector-specific planning process. • Coordinated cross-sector activities through the DHS Cyber Working Group.
Identify, Assess, and Respond to Unanticipated Infrastructure Cascading Effects During and Following Incidents	• Developed incident response best practices guidance and exercises for sector partners through the roadmap.
Strengthen Coordinated Development and Delivery of Technical Assistance, Training, and Education	• Promoted guidance such as NRC 10 CFR 73.54 and the Roadmap to Enhance Cyber Systems Security in the Nuclear Sector (Roadmap) to help identify risk management strategies in the Nuclear Sector. • Participated as co-chair of the Nuclear Sector Joint Cyber Sub-council with sector partners to lead participation in sub council activities and provide meaningful feedback on future activities intended to enhance the sector's security and resilience. • Participated as co-chair of the Nuclear Sector Joint Cyber Sub-council in analysis ofthe National Institute of Standards and Technology's (NIST) Framework for Improving Critical Infrastructure Cybersecurity with the Roadmap and NRC 10 CFR 73.54 to identify any potential gaps.

Call to Action steps	Activities for the sector
	• Drafted nuclear sector-specific implementation guide to make NIST's Framework Cybersecurity for Improving Critical Infrastructure Cybersecurity more relatable to sector stakeholders.
Improve Critical Infrastructure Security and Resilience by Advancing Research and Development Solutions	• Established a Joint Research and Development Working Group in January 2010 to set sector research and development priorities and provide a multi-agency forum for sector partners to share research and development-related activities.
Focus on Outcomes	
Learn and Adapt During and After Exercises and Incidents	• Developed and participated in sector-specific, as well as national level, cross-sector exercises to foster preparedness and increase effective response during an incident including TOPOFF-4, the 2009 National Level Exercise, and Cyberstorm II. • Worked with sector partners to identify and share lessons learned and best practices.

Source: GAO analysis of agency information. | GAO-16-79

[a] The nuclear joint Cyber Sub-council was established by the Nuclear government coordinating council and the Nuclear sector coordinating council as a means to coordinate and collaborate on cyber matters in the Nuclear Sector.

Table 22. Transportation Systems Sector Cyber Risk Mitigation Activities

Sector-specific agencies: Department of Homeland Security (DHS) and Department of Transportation (DOT)	
Call to Action steps	**Activities for the sector**
Build Upon Partnerships	
Determine Collective Actions through Joint Planning Efforts	• Described the sector's emphasis on improving assessments of cyber components and vulnerabilities that may impact critical operations or the transportation systems as a whole in the 2010 transportation systems sector-specific plan.
Empower Local and Regional Partnerships to Build Capacity Nationally	• Assessed risk using the Transportation Sector Security Risk Assessment tool developed by the Transportation Security Administration (TSA).

Table 22. (Continued)

Call to Action steps	Activities for the sector
	• Used the Maritime Security Risk Analysis Model and other inputs to provide maritime risk information to the Transportation Sector Security Risk Assessment. • Coordinated preparedness activities among the sector's partners to prevent, protect against, respond to, and recover from all hazards. For example, SSA officials stated that they collaborated to develop scenarios for the cross-modal exercise they hosted, using the National Cybersecurity and Communications Integration Center (NCCIC) Cyber Playbook.[a]
Leverage Incentives to Advance Security and Resilience	• Promoted and incentivized cybersecurity within the maritime subsector using the Port Security Grant Program, which awarded 100 million dollars in fiscal year 2014 to assist the nation's critical infrastructure in strengthening security.
Innovate in Managing Risk	
Enable Risk-Informed Decision Making through Enhanced Situational Awareness	• Used coordination mechanisms to exchange information on its cybersecurity initiatives, including the Cross-Sector Cyber Security Working Group and Industrial Control Systems Joint Working Group. • Provided classified and unclassified information to sector partners to increase situational awareness and solicit immediate action. • Coordinated cyber protection efforts with the United States Computer Emergency Readiness Team through notifications of incidents affecting the sector and by reviewing security bulletins distributed by United States Computer Emergency Readiness Team.
Analyze Infrastructure Dependencies, Interdependencies, and Associated Cascading Effects	• Participated in the Cross-Sector Cyber Security Working Group and Industrial Control systems Joint working Group with participants from all critical infrastructure sectors to facilitate discussions on sector cyber dependencies, interdependencies, and cascading effects.

Call to Action steps	Activities for the sector
Identify, Assess, and Respond to Unanticipated Infrastructure Cascading Effects During and Following Incidents	• Facilitated the flow of information to the sector during response and recovery efforts from the National Cybersecurity and Communications Integration Center. • Promoted use of DHS continuity planning assessment tools, including the CyberResilience Review[b] and Cyber Security Evaluation Tool.[c]
Strengthen Coordinated Development and Delivery of Technical Assistance, Training, and Education	• Coordinated participation in cybersecurity programs through the sector's sector and government coordinating council partnerships. • Conducted industry outreach to enhance cybersecurity awareness in the sector by promoting training and education opportunities provided by DHS and other federal agencies. • Participated in the development of the National Institute of Standards and Technology's (NIST) Framework for Improving Critical Infrastructure Cybersecurity by attending workshops. • Promoted the use of DHS technical assistance, tools, and resources provided by the Critical Infrastructure Cyber Community Voluntary Program.[d]
Improve Critical Infrastructure Security and Resilience by Advancing Research and Development Solutions	• Worked with DHS's Office of Science and Technology to contribute to research and development efforts.
Focus on Outcomes	
Learn and Adapt During and After Exercises and Incidents	• Provided security-exercise tools and services to modal operators through TSA'sIntermodal Security Training and Exercise Program and in partnership with United States Coast Guard. Tools include software for exercise design, evaluation, and tracking for a mix of tabletop, advanced tabletop and functional exercises. • Shared after action reports from I-STEP with exercise participants to update best practices and voluntary standards and promote security awareness.

Source: GAO analysis of agency information. | GAO-16-79

[a] The NCCIC Cyber Playbook helps guide the NCCIC's response to incident reports and releasing actionable cybersecurity alerts to public and private sector partners.

[b] The Cyber Resilience Review is a no-cost, voluntary, non-technical assessment to evaluate an organization's operational resilience and cybersecurity practices. It assesses enterprise programs and practices across a range of 10 domains including risk management, incident management, service continuity, and others.

[c] The Cyber Security Evaluation Tool is a Department of Homeland Security product that assists organizations in protecting their key national cyber assets. It provides users with a systematic and repeatable approach for assessing the security posture of their cyber systems and networks.

[d] The Critical Infrastructure Cyber Community (C^3) Voluntary Program is the coordination point within the federal government for critical infrastructure owners and operators interested in improving their cyber risk management processes. The program is to support industry in increasing cyber resilience, increase awareness and use of the NIST's Cybersecurity Framework, and encourage organizations to manage cybersecurity as part of an all-hazards approach to enterprise risk management.

Table 23. Water and Wastewater Systems Sector Cyber Risk Mitigation Activities

Sector-specific agency: Environmental Protection Agency (EPA)	
Call to Action steps	**Activities for the sector**
Build Upon Partnerships	
Determine Collective Actions through Joint Planning Efforts	• Developed, with the sector and government coordinating councils, the 2008 Roadmap to Secure Control Systems in the Water Sector to detail specific goals, milestones, and activities to mitigate cybersecurity risks over the next ten years. • Assisted the sector and government coordinating councils in convening the Critical Infrastructure Protection Advisory Council Water Sector Cybersecurity Strategy Workgroup to promote adoption of the National Institute of Standards and Technology's (NIST) *Framework for Improving Critical Infrastructure Cybersecurity* within the water and wastewater systems sector.[a]
Empower Local and Regional Partnerships to Build Capacity	• Held a national series of free, 1-day workshops on cybersecurity threats and response for local water and wastewater utilities and government agencies. The workshops allowed participants to propose actions to take in response to a cyber-threat scenario and identify general planning or procedural gaps in cybersecurity practices that can be corrected.

Call to Action steps	Activities for the sector
	• Worked to upgrade EPA's Vulnerability Self-Assessment Tool to provide owners and operators of water sector assets with a consistent methodology for assessing and mitigating risks, including cyber risks. • Conducted a regional exercise that reviewed water utilities' cybersecurity practices against the ISO 27001, Information Security Management standard.[b]
Leverage Incentives to Advance Security and Resilience	• None identified.
Innovate in Managing Risk	
Enable Risk-Informed Decision Making through Enhanced Situational Awareness	• Engaged with DHS's Cross Sector Cybersecurity Working Group to review and resolve specific, critical cross-sector cybersecurity issues. • Participated in quarterly meetings of the Federal Senior Leadership Council. • Promoted the Water Information Sharing and Analysis Center as the preferred mechanism for disseminating all-hazards security information, including information on cybersecurity threats, in the water sector. • Provided classified threat briefings with the Federal Bureau of Investigation and the Department of Homeland Security to members of the sector and government coordinating councils that hold security clearances.
Analyze Infrastructure Dependencies, Interdependencies, and Associated Cascading Effects	• Engaged with all partners, including DHS's Cross-Sector Cyber Security Working Group and the Industrial Control Systems Joint Working Group, to enhance identification of cyber interdependencies between sectors. • Worked with other sector-specific agencies to understand how incidents occurring in other sectors affect the water sector. For example, it was determined that the biggest threat to a water utility is the loss of power. As a result, EPA strengthened its relationship with the Department of Energy.
Identify, Assess, and Respond to Unanticipated Infrastructure Cascading Effects During and Following Incidents	• Leveraged the Water Information Sharing and Analysis Center's information sharing partnerships with the National Cybersecurity and Communication Integration Center, Industrial Control Systems Cyber Emergency Response

Table 23. (Continued)

Call to Action steps	Activities for the sector
	Team, and the Department of Defense's United States Cyber Command, to provide operational and tactical capabilities for information sharing and, in some cases, support for incident response activities. • Developed, along with the Water Research Foundation and American Water Works Association, the Business Continuity Plan Tool Kit for water utilities, which consists of a business continuity planning guide, template, and training video.
Strengthen Coordinated Development and Delivery of Technical Assistance, Training, and Education	• Developed and promoted free tools and resources for water systems to use in preparing for, responding to, and recovering from all types of hazards. • Collaborated with DHS through the Water Sector Cybersecurity Strategy Work Group to promote adoption of the National Institute of Standards and Technology Framework for Improving Critical Infrastructure Cybersecurity across the sector. • Collaborated with DHS and the FBI to deliver 1-day training courses to water and wastewater utilities on cybersecurity threat overview and response.
Improve Critical Infrastructure Security and Resilience by Advancing Research and Development Solutions	• Represented the water sector in research and development coordination across federal agencies and with critical infrastructure and key resources partners. • Contributed to development of the National Critical Infrastructure Protection Research and Development Plan as a member of the Infrastructure Subcommittee support team.
Focus on Outcomes	
Learn and Adapt During and After Exercises and Incidents	• Developed a table-top exercise tool that provides materials for utilities to plan and facilitate their own tabletop exercise focusing on water-related
	emergencies. The tool includes 15 scenarios addressing natural hazards and man-made incidents. • Worked with sector partners to support the development and deployment of tools, training, and other assistance to enhance preparedness and resiliency and leverage lessons learned from past events to constantly improve their processes.

Source: Based on GAO analysis of agency information. | GAO-16-79.

[a] The CIPAC Water Sector Cybersecurity Strategy Workgroup recommended that EPA, in coordination with DHS and other sector partners, develop approaches to outreach and training; address gaps in guidance, tools, and resources; and identify measures of success for adoption of the NIST Framework for Improving Critical Infrastructure Cybersecurity in the water sector.

[b] ISO 27001 is an information security management standard encompassing a systematic approach to managing sensitive company information, including applying a risk management process, so that the information remains secure.

End Notes

[1] The term "critical infrastructure" as defined in the Uniting and Strengthening America by Providing Appropriate Tools Required to Intercept and Obstruct Terrorism Act of 2001 (USA PATRIOT Act) refers to systems and assets so vital to the United States that their incapacity or destruction would have a debilitating impact on security, national economic security, national public health or safety, or any combination of these. 42 U.S.C. §5195c(e). Federal policy identifies 16 critical infrastructures: chemical; commercial facilities; communications; critical manufacturing; dams; defense industrial base; emergency services; energy; financial services; food and agriculture; government facilities; health care and public health; information technology; nuclear reactors, materials, and waste; transportation systems; and water and wastewater systems.

[2] See GAO, *High-Risk Series: An Update*, GAO-15-290 (Washington, D.C.: February 2015).

[3] DHS, *NIPP 2013: Partnering for Critical Infrastructure Security and Resilience*, (December 2013).

[4] White House, Presidential Policy Directive 21 (PPD 21), *Critical Infrastructure Security and Resilience* (Feb. 12, 2013).

[5] The government facilities sector was excluded due to its uniquely governmental focus.

[6] "All hazards" is defined by Presidential Policy Directive 21 as a threat or an incident, natural or manmade, that warrants action to protect life, property, the environment, and public health or safety, and to minimize disruptions of government, social, or economic activities. It includes natural disasters, cyber incidents, industrial accidents, pandemics, acts of terrorism, sabotage, and destructive criminal activity targeting critical infrastructure.

[7] The Industrial Control Systems Cyber Emergency Response Team (ICS-CERT) works to reduce risks within and across all critical infrastructure sectors by partnering with law enforcement agencies and the intelligence community and coordinating efforts among federal, state, local, and tribal governments and control systems owners, operators, and vendors. Additionally, ICS-CERT collaborates with international and private sector computer emergency response teams to share control systems-related security incidents and mitigation measures.

[8] DHS, *National Infrastructure Protection Plan–Partnering to Enhance Protection and Resiliency* (March 2009).

[9] DHS, *2014 Sector-Specific Plan Guidance–Guide for Developing a Sector-Specific Plan under NIPP 2013* (August 2014).

[10] Sector coordinating councils are self-organized and self-governed voluntary associations key stakeholders within a sector such as the owners and operators of a sector's critical assets.

[11] Government coordinating councils are comprised of representatives from federal, state, local, tribal, and territorial government entities for each sector.

[12] The NIPP presented a total of 12 steps; however, we excluded two steps that we determined did not have a cybersecurity-related nexus.

[13] Exec. Order No. 13636, 78 Fed Reg. 11,739 (Feb. 19, 2013).

[14] NIST, *Framework for Improving Critical Infrastructure Cybersecurity* (February 12, 2014).

[15] DHS, *Roadmap to Secure Controls Systems in the Chemical Sector* (September 2009).

[16] DHS, *Chemical Sector-Specific Plan* (April 2010).

[17] DHS, *2012 Risk Assessment Report for Communications* (September 27, 2012).

[18] DOD, *Report on Department of Defense Progress in Defending the Department and the Defense Industrial Base from Cyber Events* (July 8, 2011); *Report on Department of Defense Progress in Defending the Department and the Defense Industrial Base from Cyber Events* (October 9, 2012); *Report on Department of Defense Progress in Defending the Department and the Defense Industrial Base from Cyber Events* (May 24, 2013); *Report on Department of Defense Progress in Defending the Department and the Defense Industrial Base from Cyber Events for Fiscal Year 2013* (August 14, 2014); and *Report on Department of Defense Progress in Defending the Department and the Defense Industrial Base from Cyber Events for Fiscal Year 2014* (June 4, 2015).

[19] The Cybersecurity Assessment and Risk Management Approach is a DHS-developed methodology to assess cybersecurity risks using a five stage process: (1) scope risk management activities; (2) identify cyber infrastructure; (3) conduct cyber risk assessment; (4) develop cyber risk management strategy; and (5) implement strategy and measure effectiveness.

[20] DHS, *Emergency Services Sector Cyber Risk Assessment* (April 2012).

[21] GAO, *Critical Infrastructure Protection: More Comprehensive Planning Would Enhance the Cybersecurity of Public Safety Entities' Emerging Technologies*, GAO-14-125 (Washington, D.C.: Jan. 28, 2014).

[22] Pub. L. No. 104-191, Title II, Subtitle F, 110 Stat. 1936, 2021 (Aug. 21, 1996) (codified at 42 U.S.C. §§ 1320d–1320d-9). Additional privacy and security protections, breach notification requirements, and amendments to the HIPAA Privacy and Security Rules, were established by the Health Information Technology for Economic and Clinical Health Act, Pub. L. No. 111-5, Div. A, Title XIII, 123 Stat. 115, 226-279 and Div. B, Title IV, 123 Stat. 467-496 (Feb. 17, 2009).

[23] DHS, *Information Technology Sector Baseline Risk Assessment* (August 2009).

[24] Six critical functions support the IT sector's ability to produce and provide reliable IT products and maintain local and wide area networks. These critical IT sector functions are to provide (1) IT products and services; (2) incident management capabilities; (3) domain name resolution services; (4) identity management and associated trust support services; (5) Internet-based content, information, and communications services; and (6) Internet routing, access, and connection services.

[25] DHS, *Roadmap to Enhance Cyber Systems Security in the Nuclear Sector* (June 2011).

[26] DHS's Transportation Security Administration and the U.S. Coast Guard were the co- sector-specific agencies for the transportation systems sector. PPD-21 added the Department of Transportation as a co-SSA for the transportation systems sector in February 2013.

[27] DHS, *Transportation Sector Security Risk Assessment-Fiscal Year 2014 Report to Congress* (July 25, 2014).

[28] GAO, *Maritime Critical infrastructure Protection: DHS Needs to Better Address Port Cybersecurity*, GAO-14-459 (Washington, D.C.: June 5, 2014).

[29] The U.S. Coast Guard's National Maritime Strategic Risk Assessment is a biennial, cross-program, prospective assessment of risk and risk reduction as a results of Coast Guard efforts. The risk assessment is based on the evaluation of scenarios that depict diverse types of maritime risk, including safety and security. In the 2014 risk assessment, the methodology focused on cyber threats to the maritime domain.

[30] EPA, *Roadmap to a Secure & Resilient Water Sector* (May 2013).

[31] The NIPP Call to Action Step, Evaluate Progress Toward the Achievement of Goals, is discussed in a separate section of this report focused on the extent to which sector- specific agencies have established performance metrics to monitor improvements in their respective sector's cybersecurity.

[32] DOD, *Improving Cybersecurity and Resilience through Acquisition–Final Report of the Department of Defense and General Services Administration* (November 2013).

[33] DHS, *Emergency Services Sector Roadmap to Secure Voice and Data Systems* (March 2014).

[34] Department of the Treasury, *Treasury Department Report to the President on Cybersecurity Incentives Pursuant to Executive Order 13636* (August 2013).

[35] GAO, *Information Security: Bank Regulators Could Improve Examinations, Data Collection, and Information Sharing*, GAO-15-509 (Washington, D.C.: July 2, 2015).

[36] DHS, *Roadmap to Enhance Cyber Systems Security in the Nuclear Sector* (June 2011).

[37] A "tearline" refers to the practice of segregating and withholding the most sensitive portions of a document, allowing the remainder to be more widely disseminated. Tearlines are portions of an intelligence report or product that provide the substance of a more highly classified or controlled report without identifying sensitive sources, methods, or other operational information.

[38] GAO-14-459.

[39] Health Information Technology for Economic and Clinical Health (HITECH) Act, Public Law 111-5, section 13402.

[40] DHS, *Sector Outreach and Programs Division Organizational Strategy: Fiscal Year 2014-2016* (April 2014).

[41] GAO, *Communications Networks: Outcome-Based Measures Would Assist DHS in Assessing Effectiveness of Cybersecurity Efforts* (Washington, D.C.: April 3, 2013).

[42] The Financial and Banking Information Infrastructure Committee (FBIIC) is chartered under the President's Working Group on Financial Markets, and is charged with improving coordination and communication among financial regulators, enhancing the resiliency of the financial sector, and promoting the public/private partnership.

[43] 2013 NIPP Call to Action #1, Set National Focus through Jointly Developed Priorities, and Call to Action #8, Promote Infrastructure, Community, and Regional Recovery Following Incidents, were not included in our analysis of the SSAs' risk mitigation activities.

[44] The NIPP Call to Action Step, Evaluate Progress Toward the Achievement of Goals, was deferred to a later objective of the report focused on the extent to which sector-specific agencies have established performance metrics to monitor improvements in their respective sector's cybersecurity.

In: Federal Cybersecurity
Editor: Jeffery H. Matthews
ISBN: 978-1-63485-310-1

Chapter 2

PRESIDENTIAL POLICY DIRECTIVE 21: CRITICAL INFRASTRUCTURE SECURITY AND RESILIENCE*

The White House

The Presidential Policy Directive (PPD) on Critical Infrastructure Security and Resilience advances a national unity of effort to strengthen and maintain secure, functioning, and resilient critical infrastructure.

INTRODUCTION

The Nation's critical infrastructure provides the essential services that underpin American society. Proactive and coordinated efforts are necessary to strengthen and maintain secure, functioning, and resilient critical infrastructure – including assets, networks, and systems – that are vital to public confidence and the Nation's safety, prosperity, and well-being.

The Nation's critical infrastructure is diverse and complex. It includes distributed networks, varied organizational structures and operating models (including multinational ownership), interdependent functions and systems in both the physical space and cyberspace, and governance constructs that

* This is an edited, reformatted and augmented version of PPD-21, released by the White House, Office of the Press Secretary, dated February 12, 2013.

involve multi-level authorities, responsibilities, and regulations. Critical infrastructure owners and operators are uniquely positioned to manage risks to their individual operations and assets, and to determine effective strategies to make them more secure and resilient.

Critical infrastructure must be secure and able to withstand and rapidly recover from all hazards. Achieving this will require integration with the national preparedness system across prevention, protection, mitigation, response, and recovery.

This directive establishes national policy on critical infrastructure security and resilience. This endeavor is a shared responsibility among the Federal, state, local, tribal, and territorial (SLTT) entities, and public and private owners and operators of critical infrastructure (herein referred to as "critical infrastructure owners and operators"). This directive also refines and clarifies the critical infrastructure-related functions, roles, and responsibilities across the Federal Government, as well as enhances overall coordination and collaboration. The Federal Government also has a responsibility to strengthen the security and resilience of its own critical infrastructure, for the continuity of national essential functions, and to organize itself to partner effectively with and add value to the security and resilience efforts of critical infrastructure owners and operators.

POLICY

It is the policy of the United States to strengthen the security and resilience of its critical infrastructure against both physical and cyber threats. The Federal Government shall work with critical infrastructure owners and operators and SLTT entities to take proactive steps to manage risk and strengthen the security and resilience of the Nation's critical infrastructure, considering all hazards that could have a debilitating impact on national security, economic stability, public health and safety, or any combination thereof. These efforts shall seek to reduce vulnerabilities, minimize consequences, identify and disrupt threats, and hasten response and recovery efforts related to critical infrastructure.

The Federal Government shall also engage with international partners to strengthen the security and resilience of domestic critical infrastructure and critical infrastructure located outside of the United States on which the Nation depends.

U.S. efforts shall address the security and resilience of critical infrastructure in an integrated, holistic manner to reflect this infrastructure's interconnectedness and interdependency. This directive also identifies energy and communications systems as uniquely critical due to the enabling functions they provide across all critical infrastructure sectors.

Three strategic imperatives shall drive the Federal approach to strengthen critical infrastructure security and resilience:

1) Refine and clarify functional relationships across the Federal Government to advance the national unity of effort to strengthen critical infrastructure security and resilience;
2) Enable effective information exchange by identifying baseline data and systems requirements for the Federal Government; and
3) Implement an integration and analysis function to inform planning and operations decisions regarding critical infrastructure.

All Federal department and agency heads are responsible for the identification, prioritization, assessment, remediation, and security of their respective internal critical infrastructure that supports primary mission essential functions. Such infrastructure shall be addressed in the plans and execution of the requirements in the National Continuity Policy.

Federal departments and agencies shall implement this directive in a manner consistent with applicable law, Presidential directives, and Federal regulations, including those protecting privacy, civil rights, and civil liberties. In addition, Federal departments and agencies shall protect all information associated with carrying out this directive consistent with applicable legal authorities and policies.

Roles and Responsibilities

Effective implementation of this directive requires a national unity of effort pursuant to strategic guidance from the Secretary of Homeland Security. That national effort must include expertise and day-to-day engagement from the Sector-Specific Agencies (SSAs) as well as the specialized or support capabilities from other Federal departments and agencies, and strong collaboration with critical infrastructure owners and operators and SLTT entities. Although the roles and responsibilities identified in this directive are directed at Federal departments and agencies, effective partnerships with critical infrastructure owners and operators and SLTT entities are imperative to strengthen the security and resilience of the Nation's critical infrastructure.

Secretary of Homeland Security

The Secretary of Homeland Security shall provide strategic guidance, promote a national unity of effort, and coordinate the overall Federal effort to promote the security and resilience of the Nation's critical infrastructure. In carrying out the responsibilities assigned in the Homeland Security Act of 2002, as amended, the Secretary of Homeland Security evaluates national capabilities, opportunities, and challenges in protecting critical infrastructure; analyzes threats to, vulnerabilities of, and potential consequences from all hazards on critical infrastructure; identifies security and resilience functions that are necessary for effective public-private engagement with all critical infrastructure sectors; develops a national plan and metrics, in coordination with SSAs and other critical infrastructure partners; integrates and coordinates Federal cross-sector security and resilience activities; identifies and analyzes key interdependencies among critical infrastructure sectors; and reports on the effectiveness of national efforts to strengthen the Nation's security and resilience posture for critical infrastructure.

Additional roles and responsibilities for the Secretary of Homeland Security include:

1) Identify and prioritize critical infrastructure, considering physical and cyber threats, vulnerabilities, and consequences, in coordination with SSAs and other Federal departments and agencies;
2) Maintain national critical infrastructure centers that shall provide a situational awareness capability that includes integrated, actionable information about emerging trends, imminent threats, and the status of incidents that may impact critical infrastructure;
3) In coordination with SSAs and other Federal departments and agencies, provide analysis, expertise, and other technical assistance to critical infrastructure owners and operators and facilitate access to and exchange of information and intelligence necessary to strengthen the security and resilience of critical infrastructure;
4) Conduct comprehensive assessments of the vulnerabilities of the Nation's critical infrastructure in coordination with the SSAs and in

collaboration with SLTT entities and critical infrastructure owners and operators;

5) Coordinate Federal Government responses to significant cyber or physical incidents affecting critical infrastructure consistent with statutory authorities;
6) Support the Attorney General and law enforcement agencies with their responsibilities to investigate and prosecute threats to and attacks against critical infrastructure;
7) Coordinate with and utilize the expertise of SSAs and other appropriate Federal departments and agencies to map geospatially, image, analyze, and sort critical infrastructure by employing commercial satellite and airborne systems, as well as existing capabilities within other departments and agencies; and
8) Report annually on the status of national critical infrastructure efforts as required by statute.

Sector-Specific Agencies

Each critical infrastructure sector has unique characteristics, operating models, and risk profiles that benefit from an identified Sector-Specific Agency that has institutional knowledge and specialized expertise about the sector. Recognizing existing statutory or regulatory authorities of specific Federal departments and agencies, and leveraging existing sector familiarity and relationships, SSAs shall carry out the following roles and responsibilities for their respective sectors:

1) As part of the broader national effort to strengthen the security and resilience of critical infrastructure, coordinate with the Department of Homeland Security (DHS) and other relevant Federal departments and agencies and collaborate with critical infrastructure owners and operators, where appropriate with independent regulatory agencies, and with SLTT entities, as appropriate, to implement this directive;
2) Serve as a day-to-day Federal interface for the dynamic prioritization and coordination of sector-specific activities;
3) Carry out incident management responsibilities consistent with statutory authority and other appropriate policies, directives, or regulations;

4) Provide, support, or facilitate technical assistance and consultations for that sector to identify vulnerabilities and help mitigate incidents, as appropriate; and
5) Support the Secretary of Homeland Security's statutorily required reporting requirements by providing on an annual basis sector-specific critical infrastructure information.

Additional Federal Responsibilities

The following departments and agencies have specialized or support functions related to critical infrastructure security and resilience that shall be carried out by, or along with, other Federal departments and agencies and independent regulatory agencies, as appropriate.

1) The Department of State, in coordination with DHS, SSAs, and other Federal departments and agencies, shall engage foreign governments and international organizations to strengthen the security and resilience of critical infrastructure located outside the United States and to facilitate the overall exchange of best practices and lessons learned for promoting the security and resilience of critical infrastructure on which the Nation depends.
2) The Department of Justice (DOJ), including the Federal Bureau of Investigation (FBI), shall lead counterterrorism and counterintelligence investigations and related law enforcement activities across the critical infrastructure sectors. DOJ shall investigate, disrupt, prosecute, and otherwise reduce foreign intelligence, terrorist, and other threats to, and actual or attempted attacks on, or sabotage of, the Nation's critical infrastructure. The FBI also conducts domestic collection, analysis, and dissemination of cyber threat information, and shall be responsible for the operation of the National Cyber Investigative Joint Task Force (NCIJTF). The NCIJTF serves as a multi-agency national focal point for coordinating, integrating, and sharing pertinent information related to cyber threat investigations, with representation from DHS, the Intelligence Community (IC), the Department of Defense (DOD), and other agencies as appropriate. The Attorney General and the Secretary of Homeland Security shall collaborate to carry out their respective critical infrastructure missions.

3) The Department of the Interior, in collaboration with the SSA for the Government Facilities Sector, shall identify, prioritize, and coordinate the security and resilience efforts for national monuments and icons and incorporate measures to reduce risk to these critical assets, while also promoting their use and enjoyment.
4) The Department of Commerce (DOC), in collaboration with DHS and other relevant Federal departments and agencies, shall engage private sector, research, academic, and government organizations to improve security for technology and tools related to cyber-based systems, and promote the development of other efforts related to critical infrastructure to enable the timely availability of industrial products, materials, and services to meet homeland security requirements.
5) The IC, led by the Director of National Intelligence (DNI), shall use applicable authorities and coordination mechanisms to provide, as appropriate, intelligence assessments regarding threats to critical infrastructure and coordinate on intelligence and other sensitive or proprietary information related to critical infrastructure. In addition, information security policies, directives, standards, and guidelines for safeguarding national security systems shall be overseen as directed by the President, applicable law, and in accordance with that direction, carried out under the authority of the heads of agencies that operate or exercise authority over such national security systems.
6) The General Services Administration, in consultation with DOD, DHS, and other departments and agencies as appropriate, shall provide or support government-wide contracts for critical infrastructure systems and ensure that such contracts include audit rights for the security and resilience of critical infrastructure.
7) The Nuclear Regulatory Commission (NRC) is to oversee its licensees' protection of commercial nuclear power reactors and non-power nuclear reactors used for research, testing, and training; nuclear materials in medical, industrial, and academic settings, and facilities that fabricate nuclear fuel; and the transportation, storage, and disposal of nuclear materials and waste. The NRC is to collaborate, to the extent possible, with DHS, DOJ, the Department of Energy, the Environmental Protection Agency, and other Federal departments and agencies, as appropriate, on strengthening critical infrastructure security and resilience.
8) The Federal Communications Commission, to the extent permitted by law, is to exercise its authority and expertise to partner with DHS and

the Department of State, as well as other Federal departments and agencies and SSAs as appropriate, on: (1) identifying and prioritizing communications infrastructure; (2) identifying communications sector vulnerabilities and working with industry and other stakeholders to address those vulnerabilities; and (3) working with stakeholders, including industry, and engaging foreign governments and international organizations to increase the security and resilience of critical infrastructure within the communications sector and facilitating the development and implementation of best practices promoting the security and resilience of critical communications infrastructure on which the Nation depends.

9) Federal departments and agencies shall provide timely information to the Secretary of Homeland Security and the national critical infrastructure centers necessary to support cross-sector analysis and inform the situational awareness capability for critical infrastructure.

Three Strategic Imperatives

1) Refine and Clarify Functional Relationships across the Federal Government to Advance the National Unity of Effort to Strengthen Critical Infrastructure Security and Resilience

An effective national effort to strengthen critical infrastructure security and resilience must be guided by a national plan that identifies roles and responsibilities and is informed by the expertise, experience, capabilities, and responsibilities of the SSAs, other Federal departments and agencies with critical infrastructure roles, SLTT entities, and critical infrastructure owners and operators.

During the past decade, new programs and initiatives have been established to address specific infrastructure issues, and priorities have shifted and expanded. As a result, Federal functions related to critical infrastructure security and resilience shall be clarified and refined to establish baseline capabilities that will reflect this evolution of knowledge, to define relevant Federal program functions, and to facilitate collaboration and information exchange between and among the Federal Government, critical infrastructure owners and operators, and SLTT entities.

As part of this refined structure, there shall be two national critical infrastructure centers operated by DHS – one for physical infrastructure and another for cyber infrastructure. They shall function in an integrated manner and serve as focal points for critical infrastructure partners to obtain situational awareness and integrated, actionable information to protect the physical and cyber aspects of critical infrastructure. Just as the physical and cyber elements of critical infrastructure are inextricably linked, so are the vulnerabilities. Accordingly, an integration and analysis function (further developed in Strategic Imperative 3) shall be implemented between these two national centers.

The success of these national centers, including the integration and analysis function, is dependent on the quality and timeliness of the information and intelligence they receive from the SSAs and other Federal departments and agencies, as well as from critical infrastructure owners and operators and SLTT entities.

These national centers shall not impede the ability of the heads of Federal departments and agencies to carry out or perform their responsibilities for national defense, criminal, counterintelligence, counterterrorism, or investigative activities.

2) Enable Efficient Information Exchange by Identifying Baseline Data and Systems Requirements for the Federal Government

A secure, functioning, and resilient critical infrastructure requires the efficient exchange of information, including intelligence, between all levels of governments and critical infrastructure owners and operators. This must facilitate the timely exchange of threat and vulnerability information as well as information that allows for the development of a situational awareness capability during incidents. The goal is to enable efficient information exchange through the identification of requirements for data and information formats and accessibility, system interoperability, and redundant systems and alternate capabilities should there be a disruption in the primary systems.

Greater information sharing within the government and with the private sector can and must be done while respecting privacy and civil liberties. Federal departments and agencies shall ensure that all existing privacy principles, policies, and procedures are implemented consistent with applicable law and policy and shall include senior agency officials for privacy in their efforts to govern and oversee information sharing properly.

3) Implement an Integration and Analysis Function to Inform Planning and Operational Decisions Regarding Critical Infrastructure

The third strategic imperative builds on the first two and calls for the implementation of an integration and analysis function for critical infrastructure that includes operational and strategic analysis on incidents, threats, and emerging risks. It shall reside at the intersection of the two national centers as identified in Strategic Imperative 1, and it shall include the capability to collate, assess, and integrate vulnerability and consequence information with threat streams and hazard information to:

a. Aid in prioritizing assets and managing risks to critical infrastructure;
b. Anticipate interdependencies and cascading impacts;
c. Recommend security and resilience measures for critical infrastructure prior to, during, and after an event or incident; and
d. Support incident management and restoration efforts related to critical infrastructure.

This function shall not replicate the analysis function of the IC or the National Counterterrorism Center, nor shall it involve intelligence collection activities. The IC, DOD, DOJ, DHS, and other Federal departments and agencies with relevant intelligence or information shall, however, inform this integration and analysis capability regarding the Nation's critical infrastructure by providing relevant, timely, and appropriate information to the national centers. This function shall also use information and intelligence provided by other critical infrastructure partners, including SLTT and nongovernmental analytic entities.

Finally, this integration and analysis function shall support DHS's ability to maintain and share, as a common Federal service, a near real-time situational awareness capability for critical infrastructure that includes actionable information about imminent threats, significant trends, and awareness of incidents that may affect critical infrastructure.

INNOVATION AND RESEARCH AND DEVELOPMENT

The Secretary of Homeland Security, in coordination with the Office of Science and Technology Policy (OSTP), the SSAs, DOC, and other Federal departments and agencies, shall provide input to align those Federal and Federally-funded research and development (R&D) activities that seek to strengthen the security and resilience of the Nation's critical infrastructure, including:

1) Promoting R&D to enable the secure and resilient design and construction of critical infrastructure and more secure accompanying cyber technology;
2) Enhancing modeling capabilities to determine potential impacts on critical infrastructure of an incident or threat scenario, as well as cascading effects on other sectors;
3) Facilitating initiatives to incentivize cybersecurity investments and the adoption of critical infrastructure design features that strengthen all-hazards security and resilience; and
4) Prioritizing efforts to support the strategic guidance issued by the Secretary of Homeland Security.

IMPLEMENTATION OF THE DIRECTIVE

The Secretary of Homeland Security shall take the following actions as part of the implementation of this directive.

1) Critical Infrastructure Security and Resilience Functional Relationships

Within 120 days of the date of this directive, the Secretary of Homeland Security shall develop a description of the functional relationships within DHS and across the Federal Government related to critical infrastructure security and resilience. It should include the roles and functions of the two national critical infrastructure centers and a discussion of the analysis and integration function. When complete, it should serve as a roadmap for critical infrastructure owners and operators and SLTT entities to navigate the Federal Government's functions and primary points of contact assigned to those functions for critical infrastructure security and resilience against both physical and cyber threats. The Secretary shall coordinate this effort with the SSAs and other relevant Federal departments and agencies. The Secretary shall provide the description to the President through the Assistant to the President for Homeland Security and Counterterrorism.

2) Evaluation of the Existing Public-Private Partnership Model

Within 150 days of the date of this directive, the Secretary of Homeland Security, in coordination with the SSAs, other relevant Federal departments and agencies, SLTT entities, and critical infrastructure owners and operators, shall conduct an analysis of the existing public-private partnership model and recommend options for improving the effectiveness of the partnership in both the physical and cyber space. The evaluation shall consider options to streamline processes for collaboration and exchange of information and to minimize duplication of effort. Furthermore, the analysis shall consider how the model can be flexible and adaptable to meet the unique needs of individual sectors while providing a focused, disciplined, and effective approach for the Federal Government to coordinate with the critical infrastructure owners and operators and with SLTT governments. The evaluation shall result in recommendations to enhance partnerships to be approved for implementation through the processes established in the Organization of the National Security Council System directive.

3) Identification of Baseline Data and Systems Requirements for the Federal Government to Enable Efficient Information Exchange

Within 180 days of the date of this directive, the Secretary of Homeland Security, in coordination with the SSAs and other Federal departments and agencies, shall convene a team of experts to identify baseline data and systems requirements to enable the efficient exchange of information and intelligence relevant to strengthening the security and resilience of critical infrastructure. The experts should include representatives from those entities that routinely possess information important to critical infrastructure security and resilience; those that determine and manage information technology systems used to exchange information; and those responsible for the security of information being exchanged. Interoperability with critical infrastructure partners; identification of key data and the information requirements of key Federal, SLTT, and private sector entities; availability, accessibility, and formats of data; the ability to exchange various classifications of information; and the security of those systems to be used; and appropriate protections for individual privacy and civil liberties should be included in the analysis. The analysis should result in baseline requirements for sharing of data and interoperability of systems to enable the timely exchange of data and information to secure critical infrastructure and make it more resilient. The Secretary shall provide that analysis to the President through the Assistant to the President for Homeland Security and Counterterrorism.

4) Development of a Situational Awareness Capability for Critical Infrastructure

Within 240 days of the date of this directive, the Secretary of Homeland Security shall demonstrate a near real-time situational awareness capability for critical infrastructure that includes threat streams and all-hazards information as well as vulnerabilities; provides the status of critical infrastructure and potential cascading effects; supports decision making; and disseminates critical information that may be needed to save or sustain lives, mitigate damage, or reduce further degradation of a critical infrastructure capability throughout an incident. This capability should be available for and cover physical and cyber elements of critical infrastructure, and enable an integration of information as necessitated by the incident.

5) Update to National Infrastructure Protection Plan

Within 240 days of the date of this directive, the Secretary of Homeland Security shall provide to the President, through the Assistant to the President for Homeland Security and Counterterrorism, a successor to the National Infrastructure Protection Plan to address the implementation of this directive, the requirements of Title II of the Homeland Security Act of 2002 as amended, and alignment with the National Preparedness Goal and System required by PPD-8. The plan shall include the identification of a risk management framework to be used to strengthen the security and resilience of critical infrastructure; the methods to be used to prioritize critical infrastructure; the protocols to be used to synchronize communication and actions within the Federal Government; and a metrics and analysis process to be used to measure the Nation's ability to manage and reduce risks to critical infrastructure. The updated plan shall also reflect the identified functional relationships within DHS and across the Federal Government and the updates to the public-private partnership model. Finally, the plan should consider sector dependencies on energy and communications systems, and identify pre-event and mitigation measures or alternate capabilities during disruptions to those systems. The Secretary shall coordinate this effort with the SSAs, other relevant Federal departments and agencies, SLTT entities, and critical infrastructure owners and operators.

6) National Critical Infrastructure Security and Resilience R&D Plan

Within 2 years of the date of this directive, the Secretary of Homeland Security, in coordination with the OSTP, the SSAs, DOC, and other Federal departments and agencies, shall provide to the President, through the Assistant to the President for Homeland Security and Counterterrorism, a National Critical Infrastructure Security and Resilience R&D Plan that takes into account the evolving threat landscape, annual metrics, and other relevant information to identify priorities and guide R&D requirements and investments. The plan should be issued every 4 years after its initial delivery, with interim updates as needed.

Policy coordination, dispute resolution, and periodic in-progress reviews for the implementation of this directive shall be carried out consistent with PPD-1, including the use of Interagency Policy Committees coordinated by the National Security Staff.

Nothing in this directive alters, supersedes, or impedes the authorities of Federal departments and agencies, including independent regulatory agencies, to carry out their functions and duties consistent with applicable legal authorities and other Presidential guidance and directives, including, but not limited to, the designation of critical infrastructure under such authorities.

This directive revokes Homeland Security Presidential Directive/HSPD-7, Critical Infrastructure Identification, Prioritization, and Protection, issued December 17, 2003. Plans developed pursuant to HSPD-7 shall remain in effect until specifically revoked or superseded.

DESIGNATED CRITICAL INFRASTRUCTURE SECTORS AND SECTOR-SPECIFIC AGENCIES

This directive identifies 16 critical infrastructure sectors and designates associated Federal SSAs. In some cases co-SSAs are designated where those departments share the roles and responsibilities of the SSA. The Secretary of Homeland Security shall periodically evaluate the need for and approve changes to critical infrastructure sectors and shall consult with the Assistant to the President for Homeland Security and Counterterrorism before changing a critical infrastructure sector or a designated SSA for that sector. The sectors and SSAs are as follows:

Chemical:
Sector-Specific Agency: Department of Homeland Security

Commercial Facilities:
Sector-Specific Agency: Department of Homeland Security

Communications:
Sector-Specific Agency: Department of Homeland Security

Critical Manufacturing:
Sector-Specific Agency: Department of Homeland Security

Dams:
Sector-Specific Agency: Department of Homeland Security

Defense Industrial Base:
Sector-Specific Agency: Department of Defense

Emergency Services:
Sector-Specific Agency: Department of Homeland Security

Energy:
Sector-Specific Agency: Department of Energy

Financial Services:
Sector-Specific Agency: Department of the Treasury

Food and Agriculture:
Co-Sector-Specific Agencies: U.S. Department of Agriculture and Department of Health and Human Services

Government Facilities:
Co-Sector-Specific Agencies: Department of Homeland Security and General Services Administration

Healthcare and Public Health:
Sector-Specific Agency: Department of Health and Human Services

Information Technology:
Sector-Specific Agency: Department of Homeland Security

Nuclear Reactors, Materials, and Waste:
Sector-Specific Agency: Department of Homeland Security

Transportation Systems:
Co-Sector-Specific Agencies: Department of Homeland Security and Department of Transportation

Water and Wastewater Systems:
Sector-Specific Agency: Environmental Protection Agency

DEFINITIONS

For purposes of this directive:

The term "all hazards" means a threat or an incident, natural or manmade, that warrants action to protect life, property, the environment, and public health or safety, and to minimize disruptions of government, social, or economic activities. It includes natural disasters, cyber incidents, industrial accidents, pandemics, acts of terrorism, sabotage, and destructive criminal activity targeting critical infrastructure.

The term "collaboration" means the process of working together to achieve shared goals.

The terms "coordinate" and "in coordination with" mean a consensus decision-making process in which the named coordinating department or agency is responsible for working with the affected departments and agencies to achieve consensus and a consistent course of action.

The term "critical infrastructure" has the meaning provided in section 1016(e) of the USA Patriot Act of 2001 (42 U.S.C. 5195c(e)), namely systems and assets, whether physical or virtual, so vital to the United States that the incapacity or destruction of such systems and assets would have a debilitating impact on security, national economic security, national public health or safety, or any combination of those matters.

The term "Federal departments and agencies" means any authority of the United States that is an "agency" under 44 U.S.C. 3502(1), other than those considered to be independent regulatory agencies, as defined in 44 U.S.C. 3502(5).

The term "national essential functions" means that subset of Government functions that are necessary to lead and sustain the Nation during a catastrophic emergency.

The term "primary mission essential functions" means those Government functions that must be performed in order to support or implement the performance of the national essential functions before, during, and in the aftermath of an emergency.

The term "national security systems" has the meaning given to it in the Federal Information Security Management Act of 2002 (44 U.S.C. 3542(b)).

The term "resilience" means the ability to prepare for and adapt to changing conditions and withstand and recover rapidly from disruptions. Resilience includes the ability to withstand and recover from deliberate attacks, accidents, or naturally occurring threats or incidents.

The term "Sector-Specific Agency" (SSA) means the Federal department or agency designated under this directive to be responsible for providing institutional knowledge and specialized expertise as well as leading, facilitating, or supporting the security and resilience programs and associated activities of its designated critical infrastructure sector in the all-hazards environment.

The terms "secure" and "security" refer to reducing the risk to critical infrastructure by physical means or defense cyber measures to intrusions, attacks, or the effects of natural or manmade disasters.

INDEX

D

E

F

G

N

O

P

R

S

T

U

V

W